You may be leaving London but I made sure that you take it with you ♡ *Ellie*

GW00372511

LONDON
Create your world

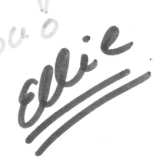

Bella

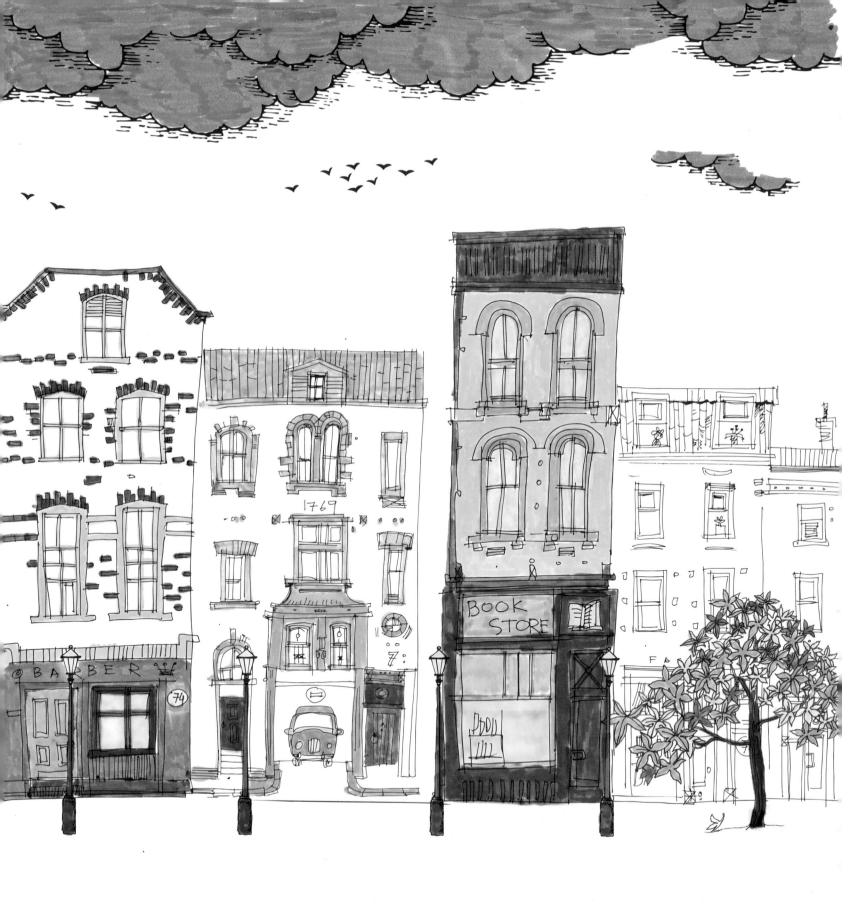

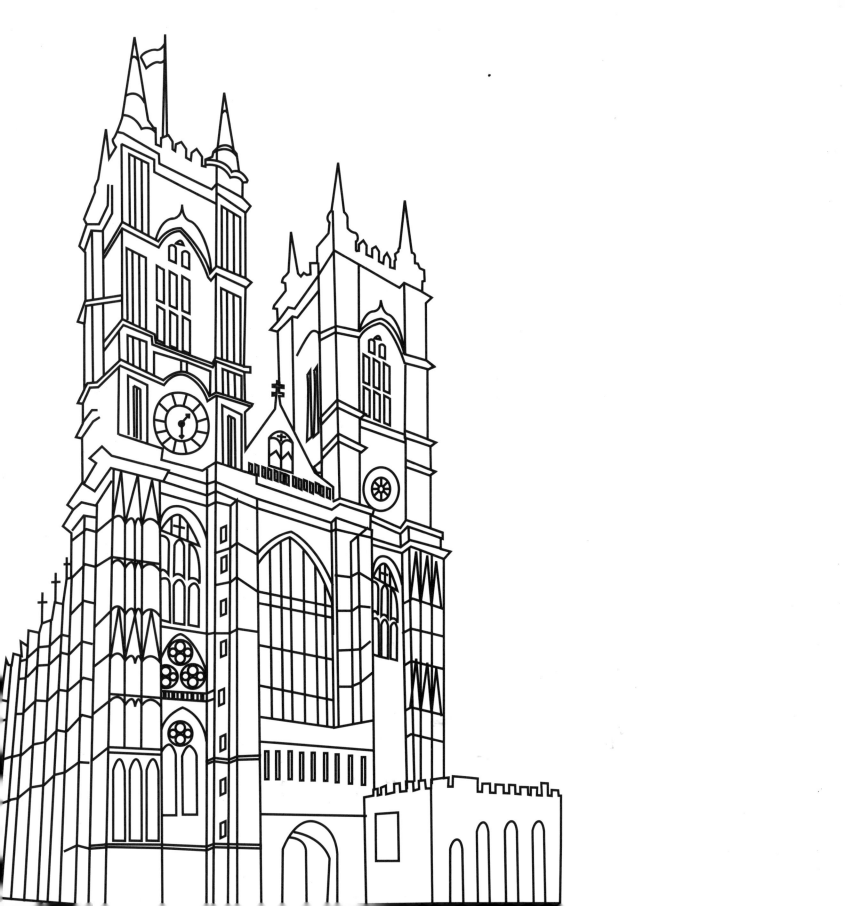

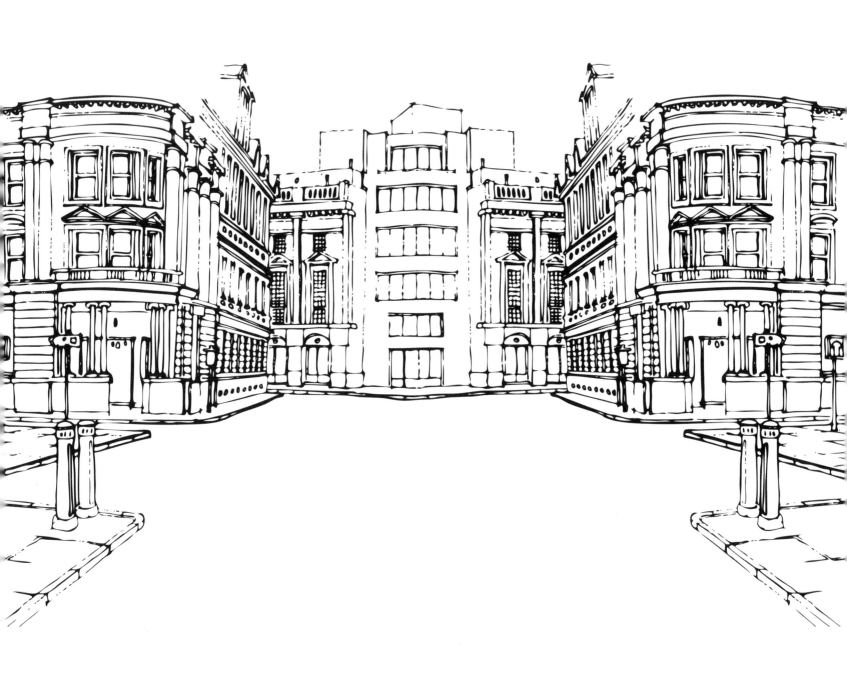

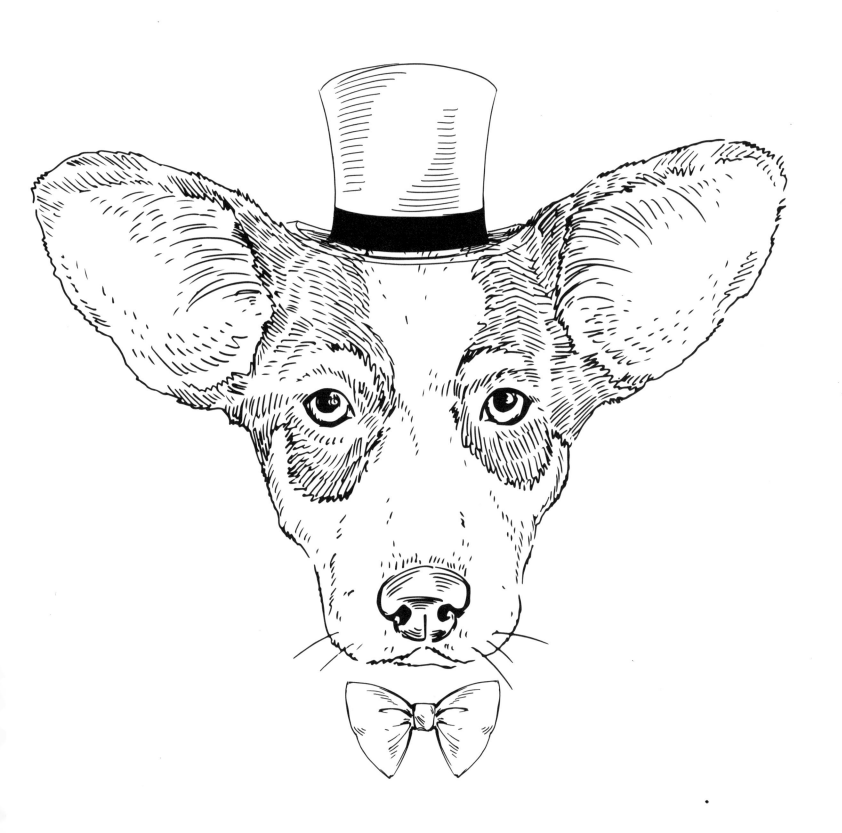

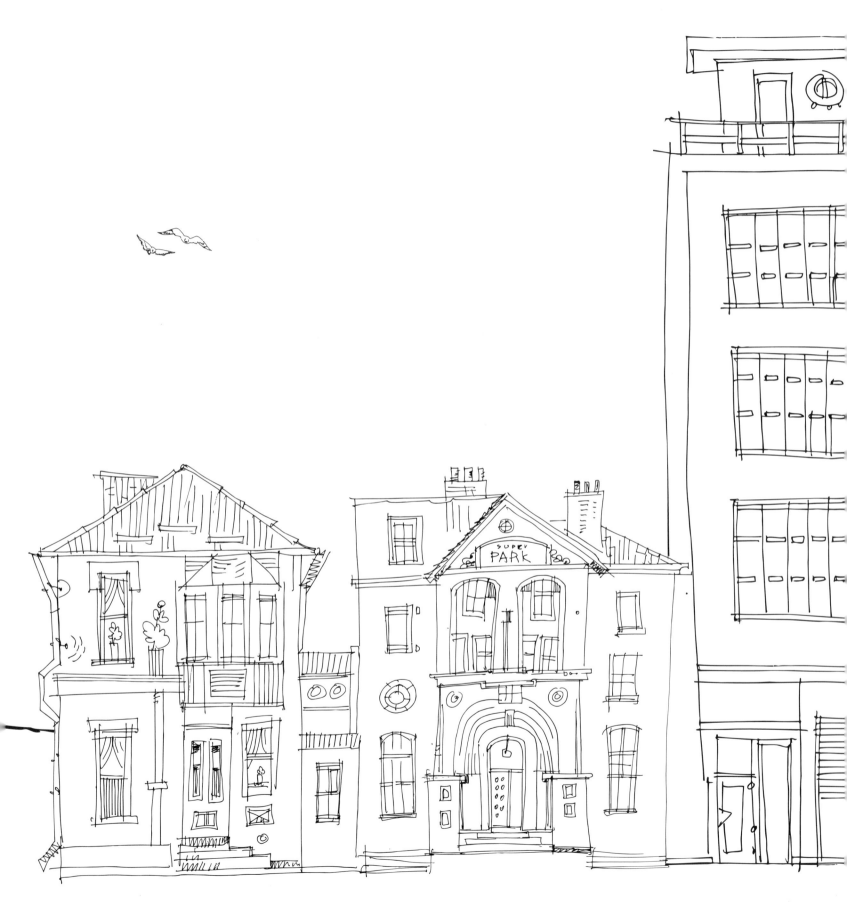

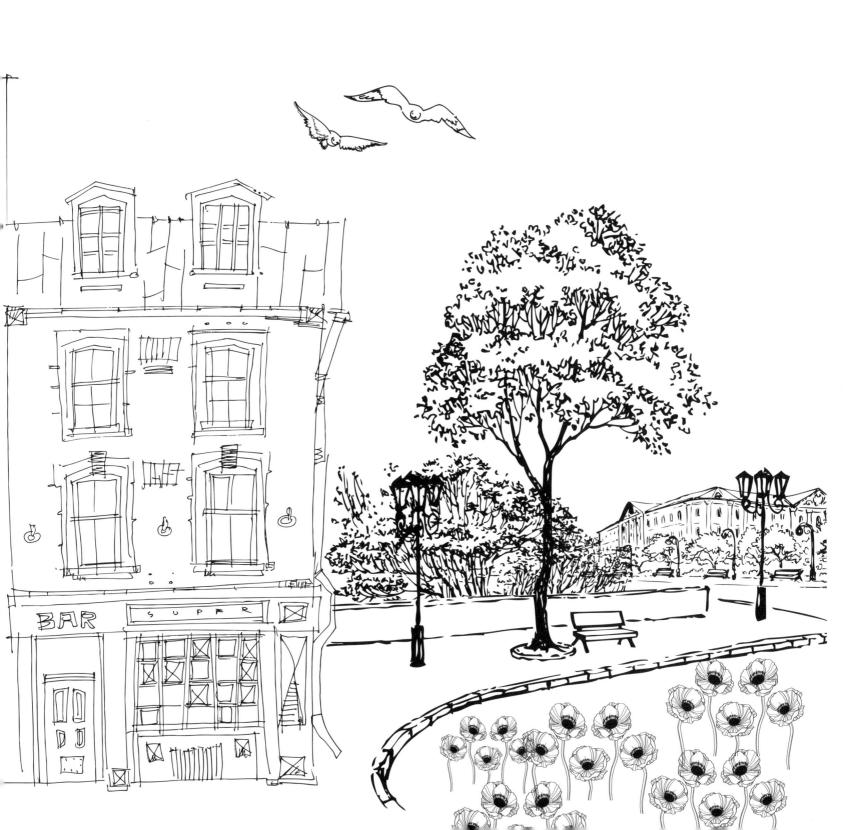

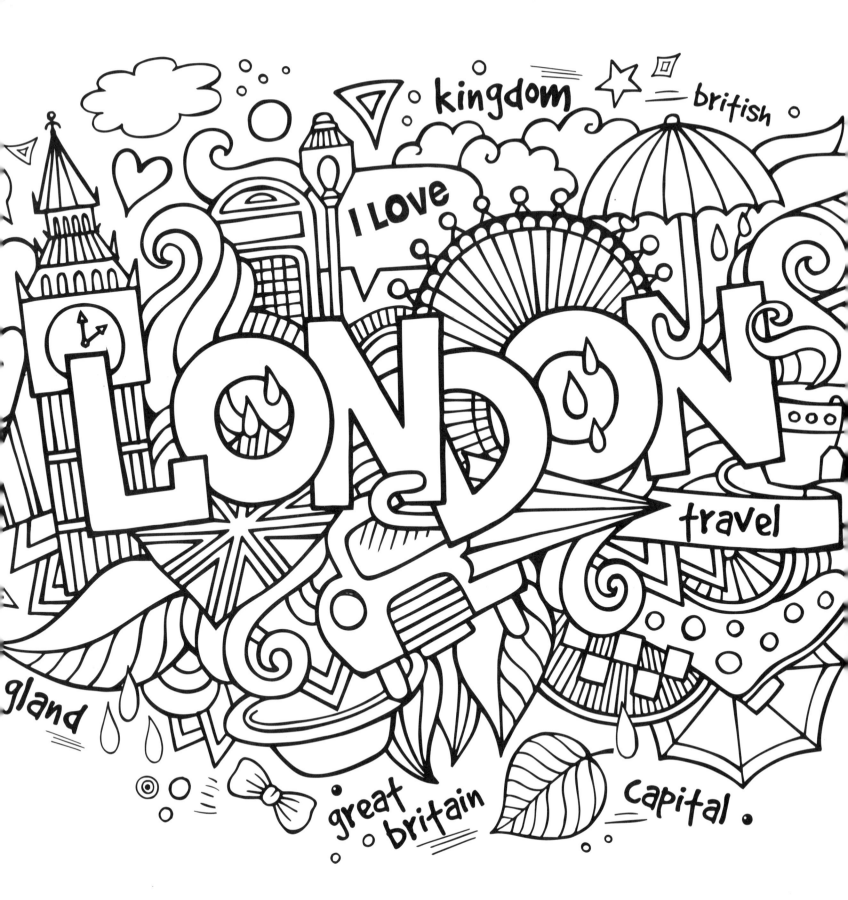

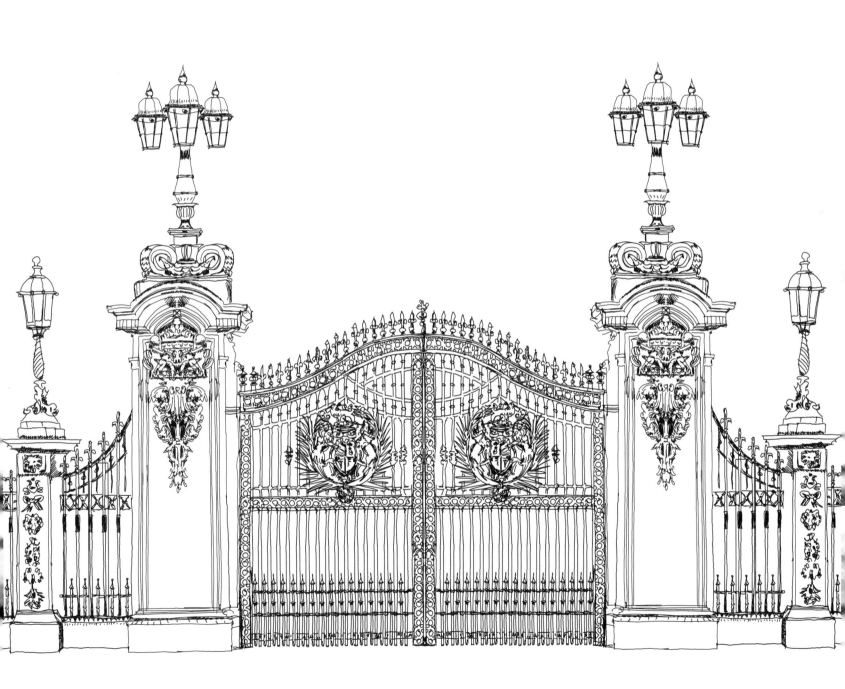

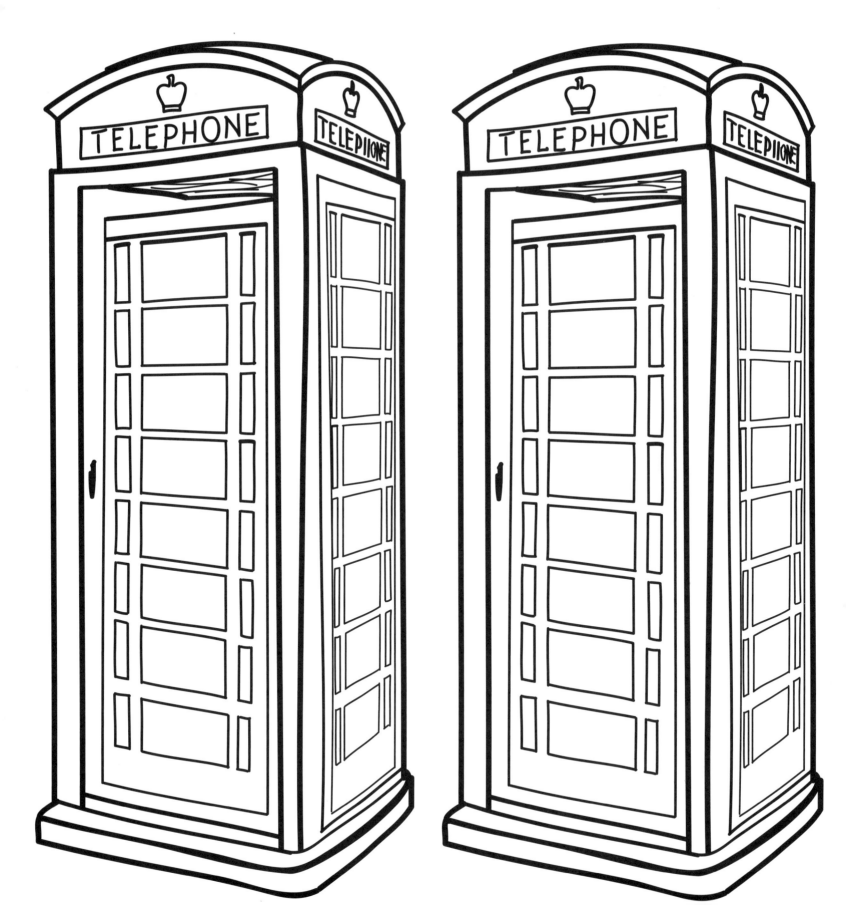

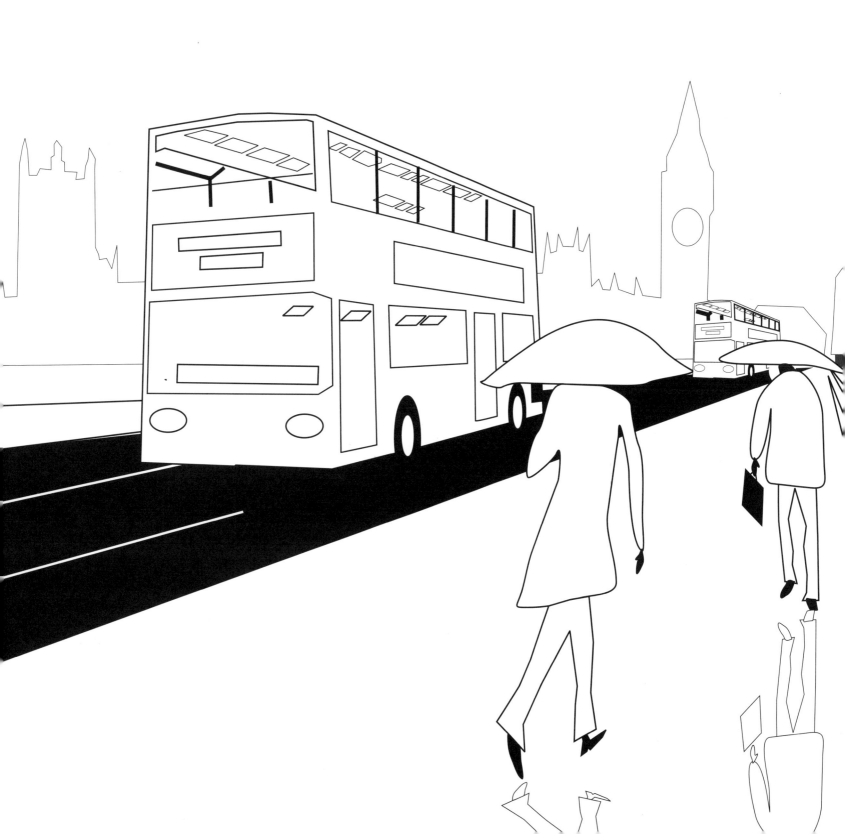

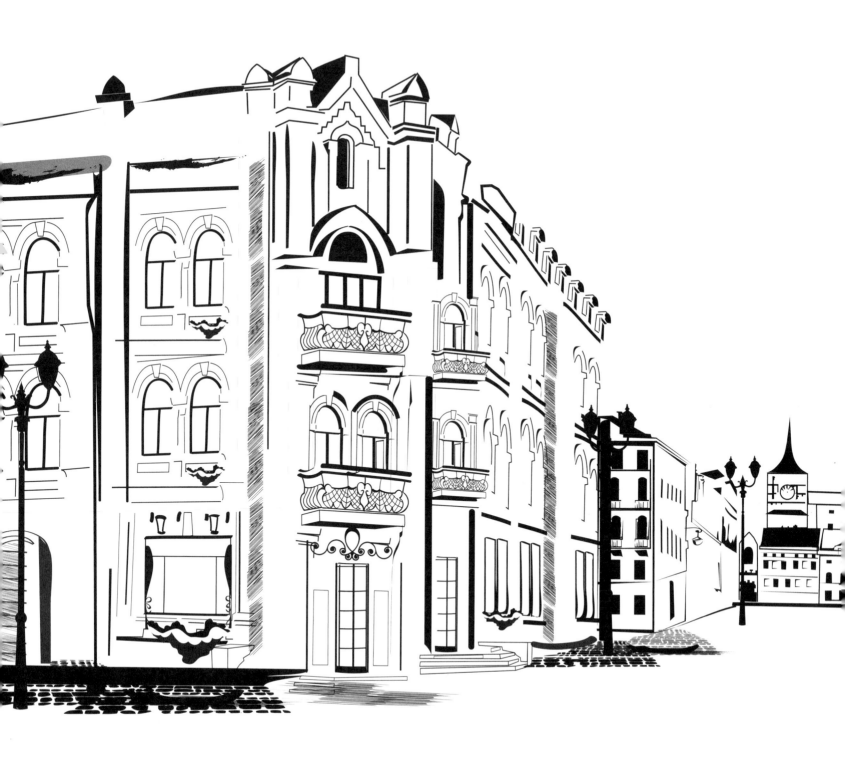

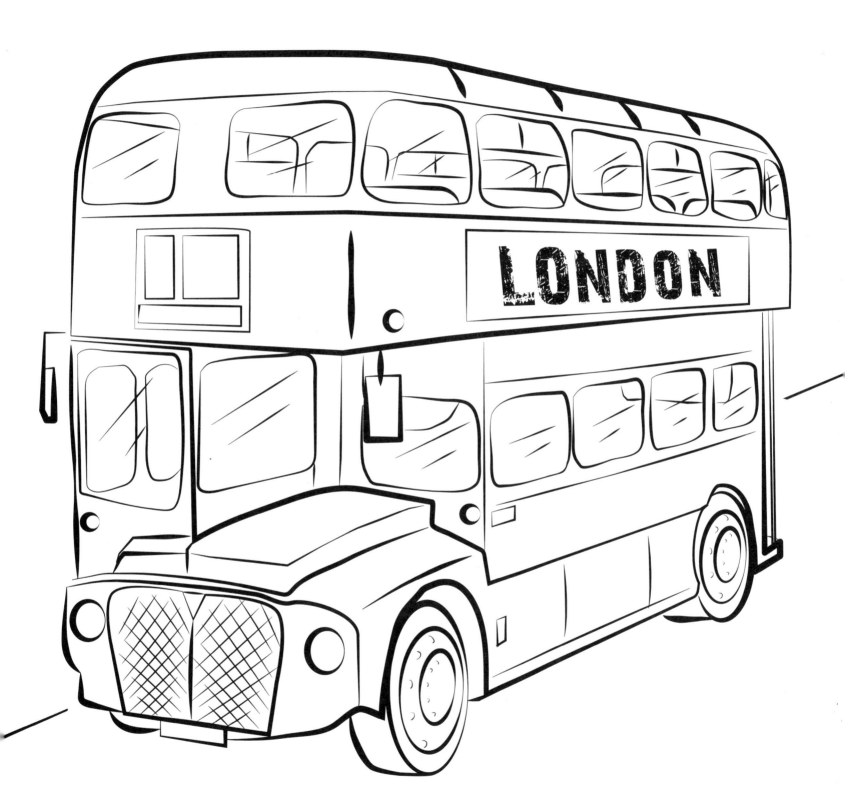

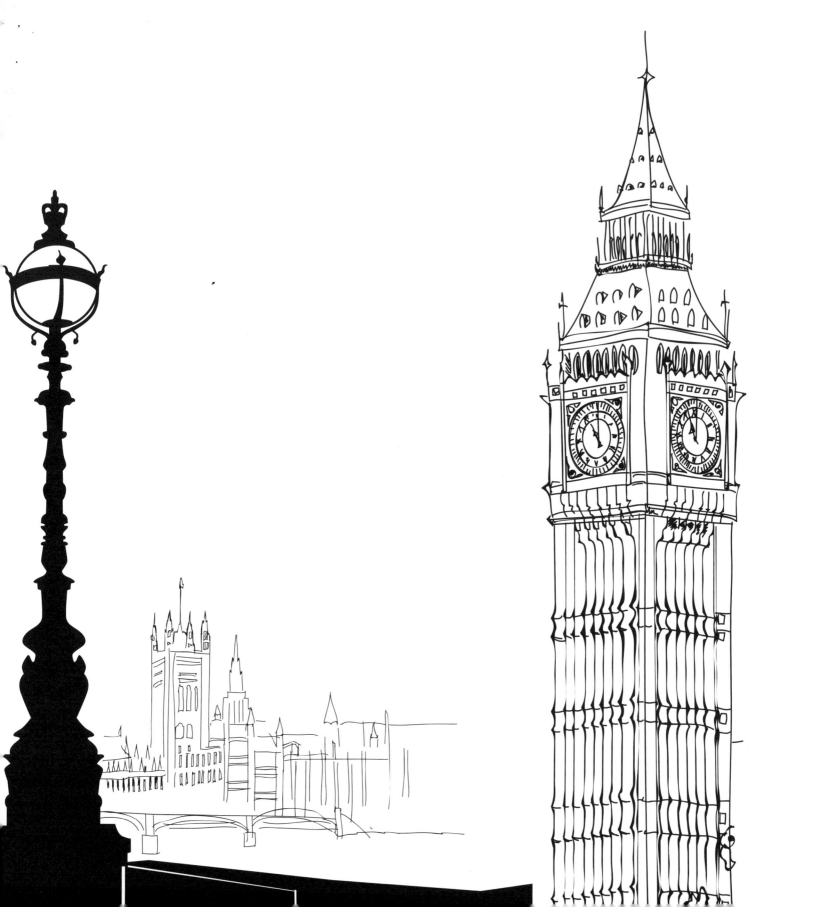

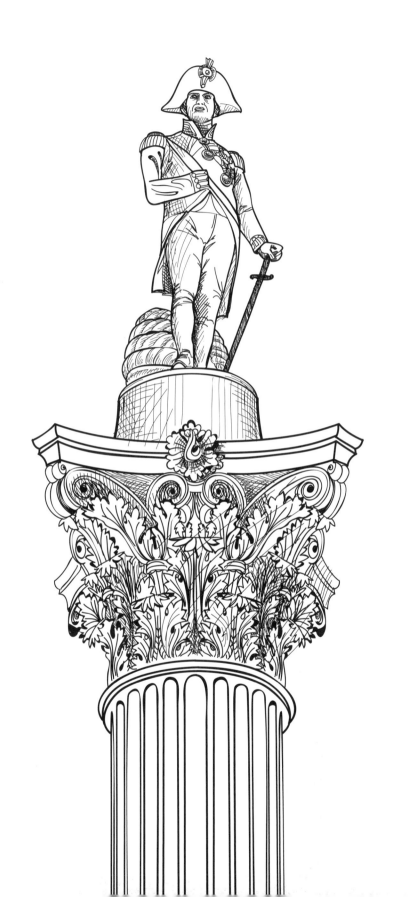

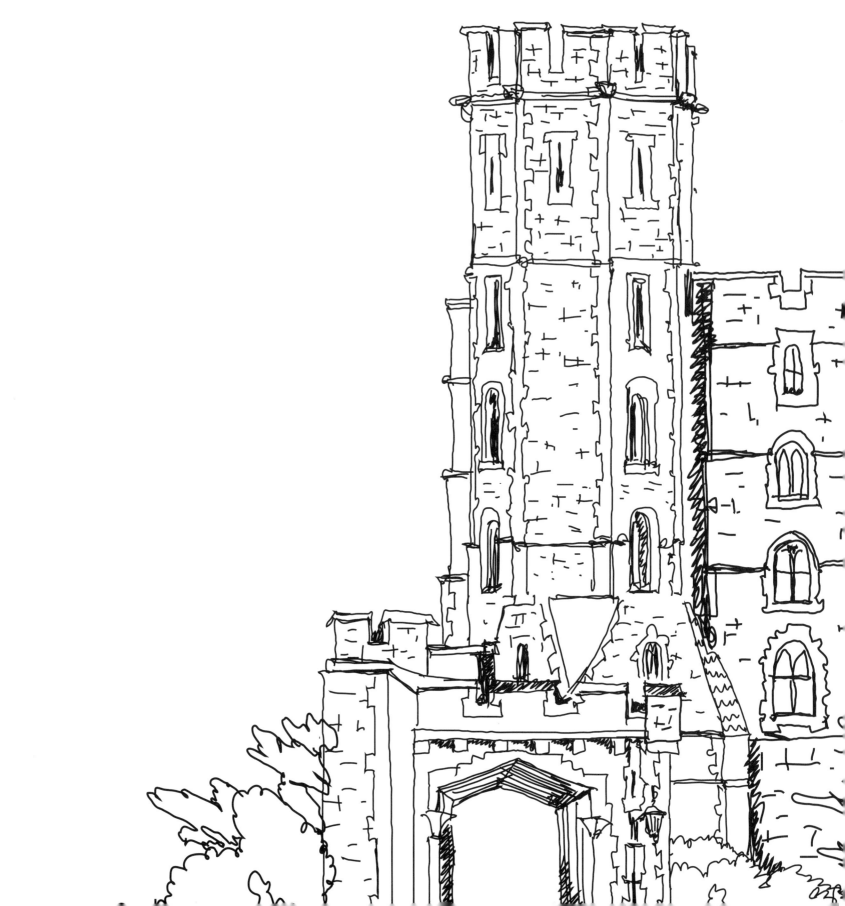

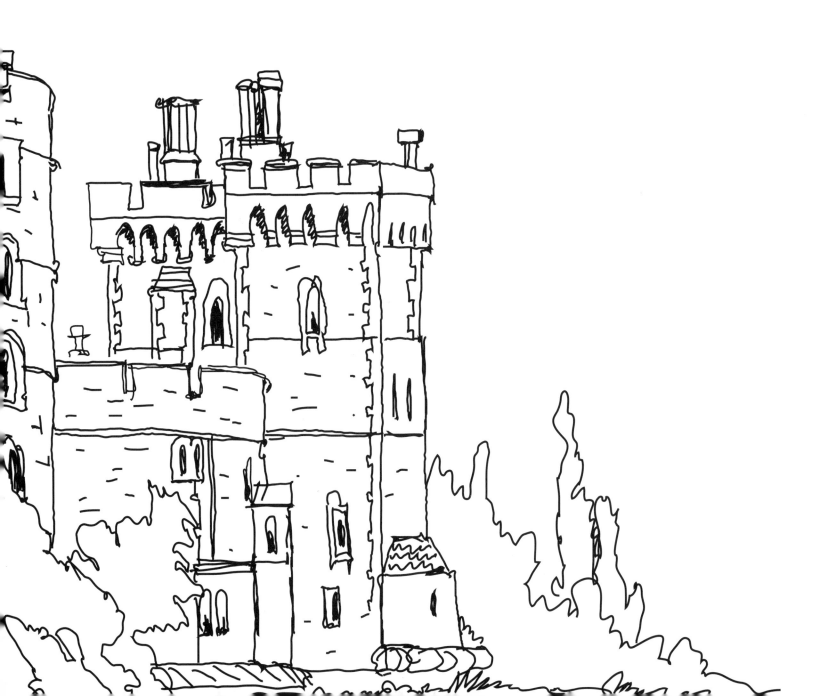

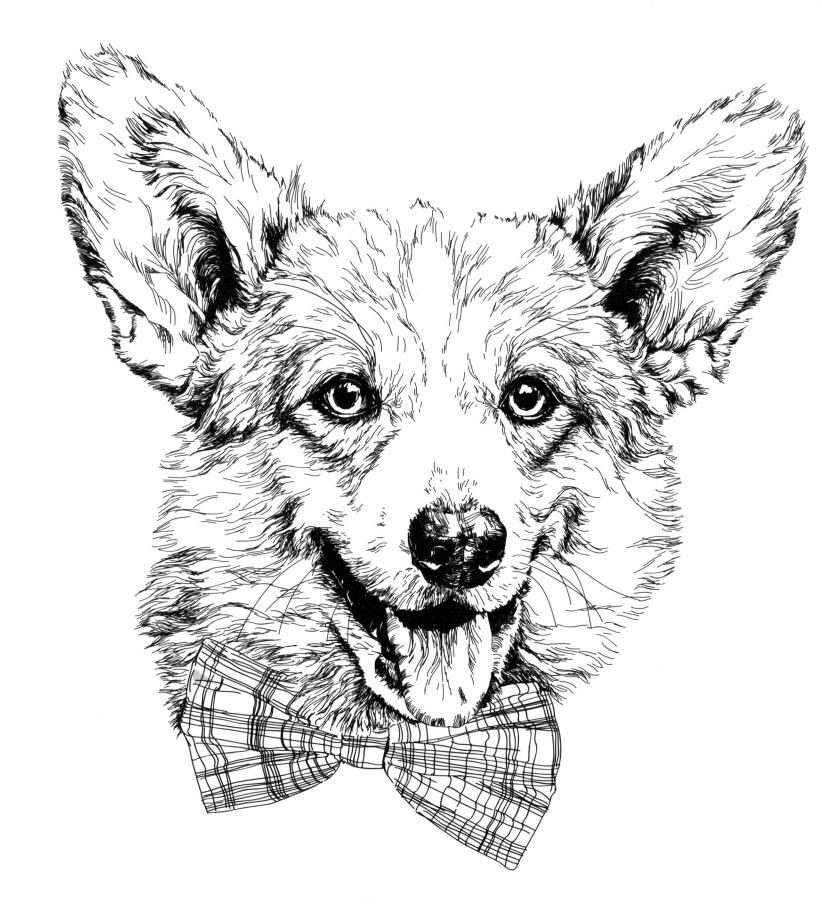

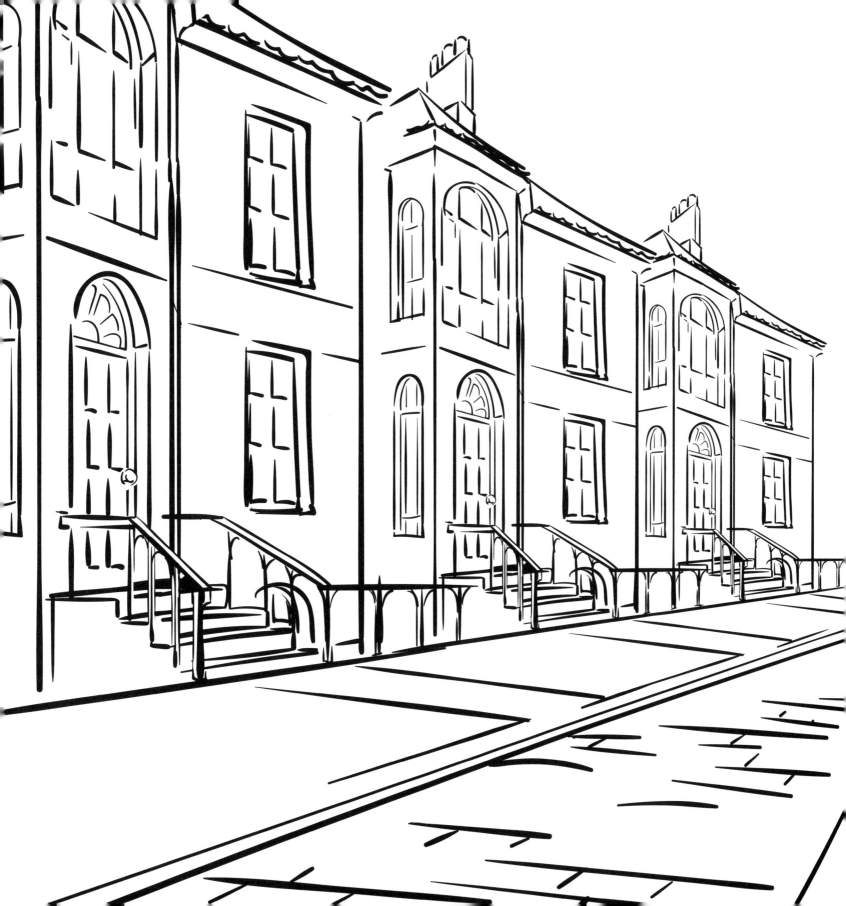

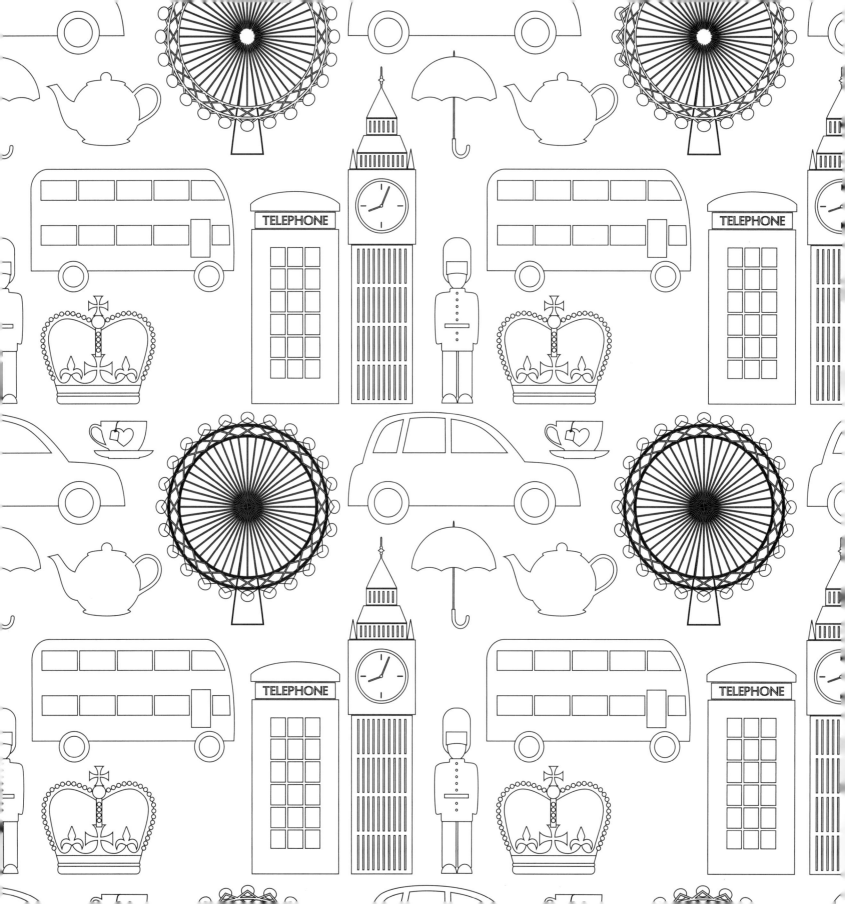

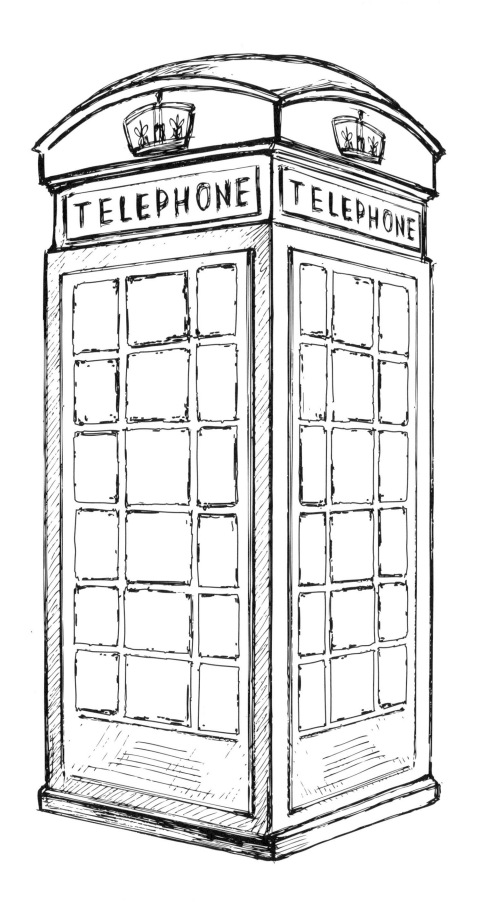

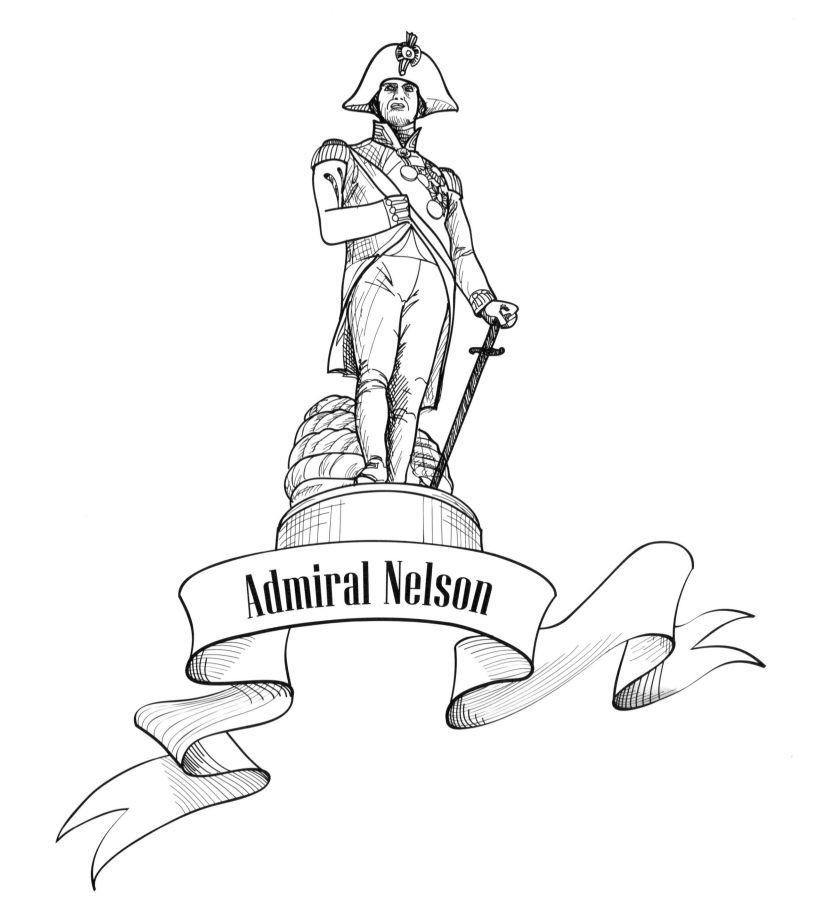

Admiral Nelson

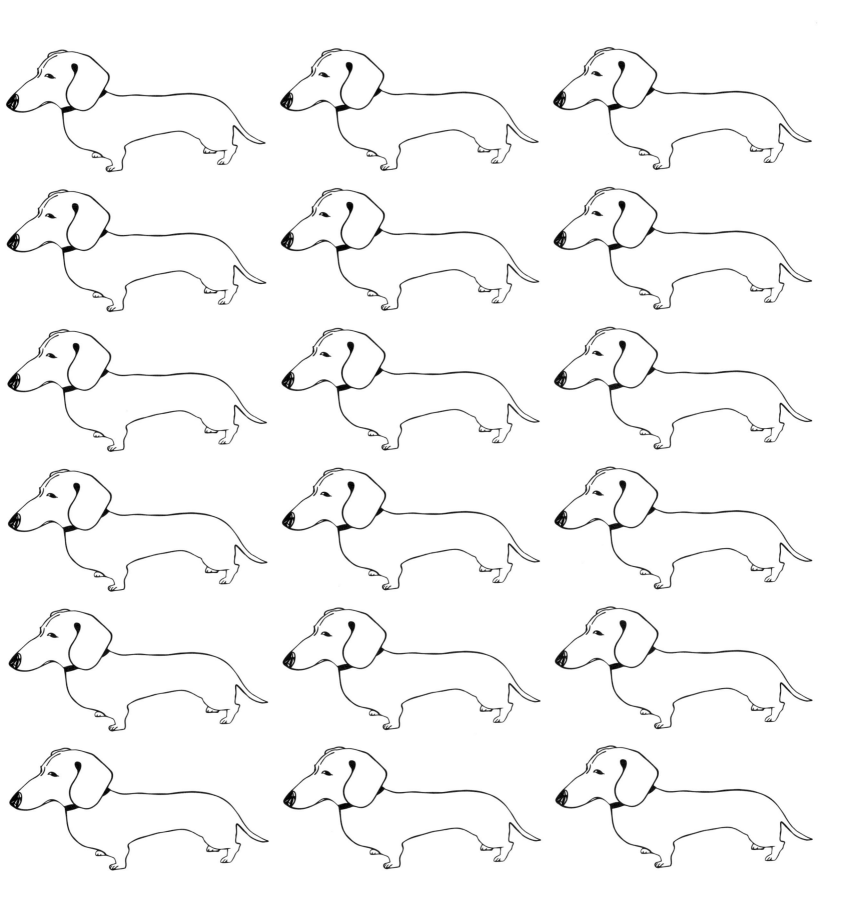

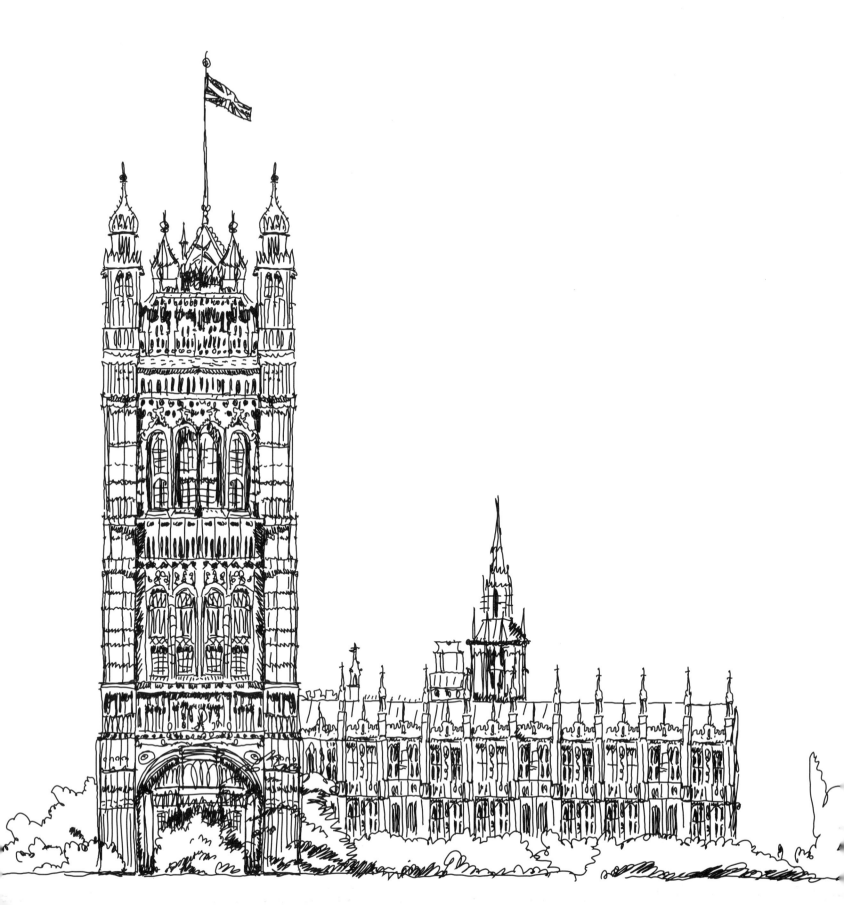

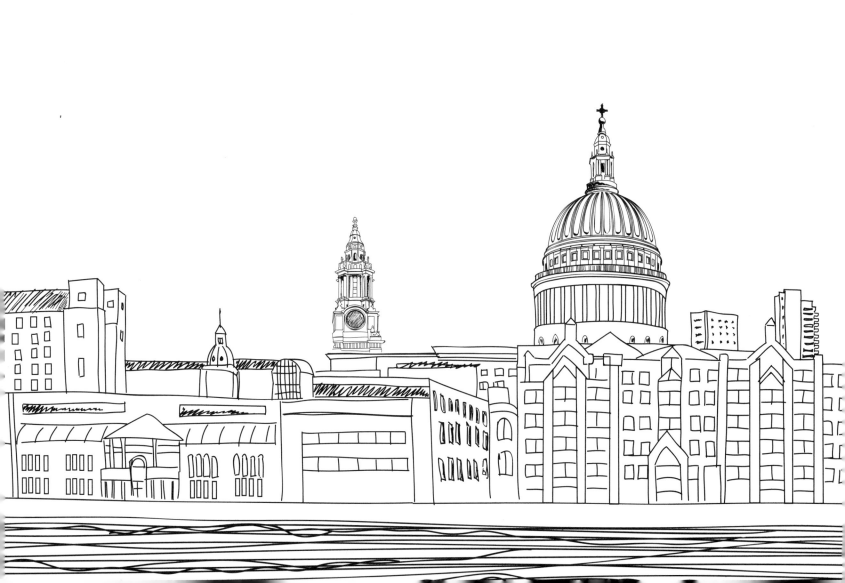

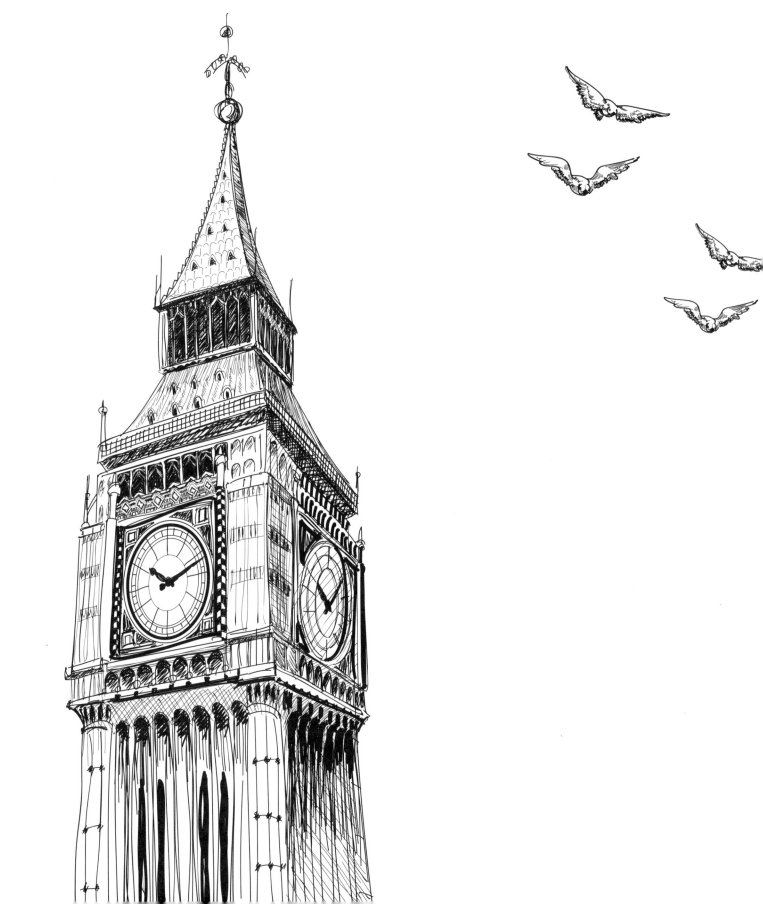

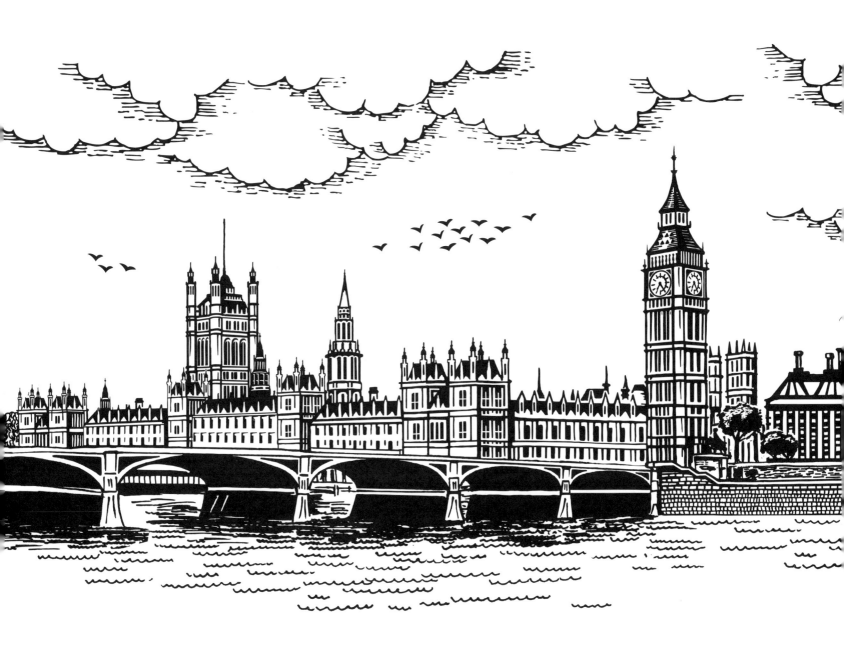

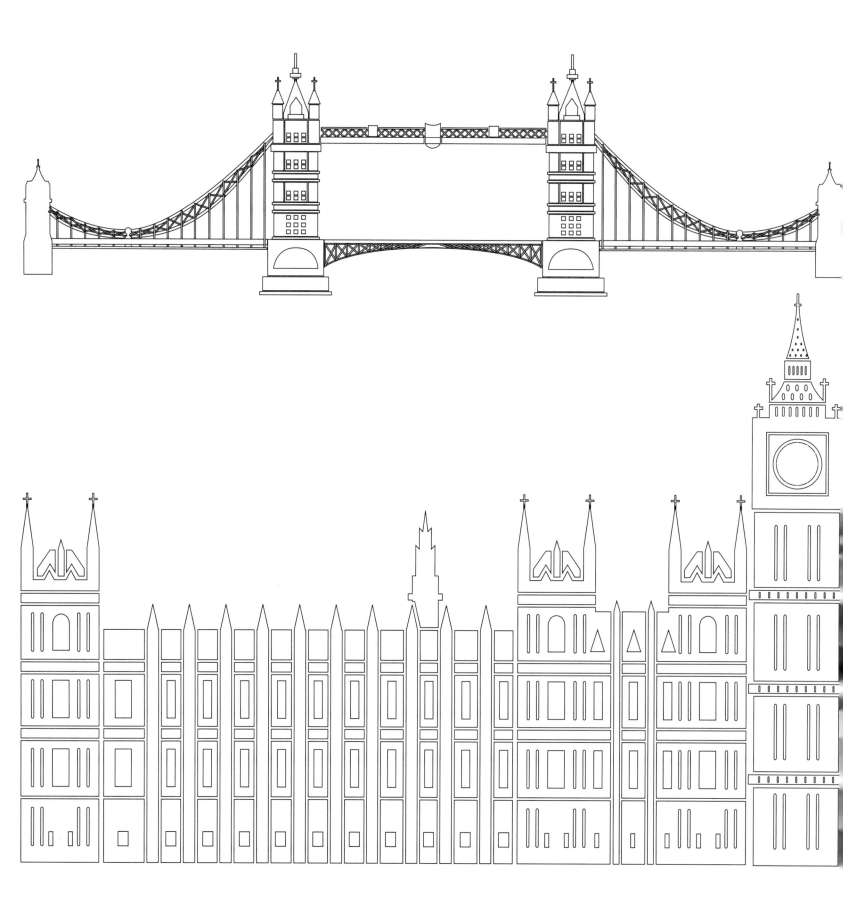

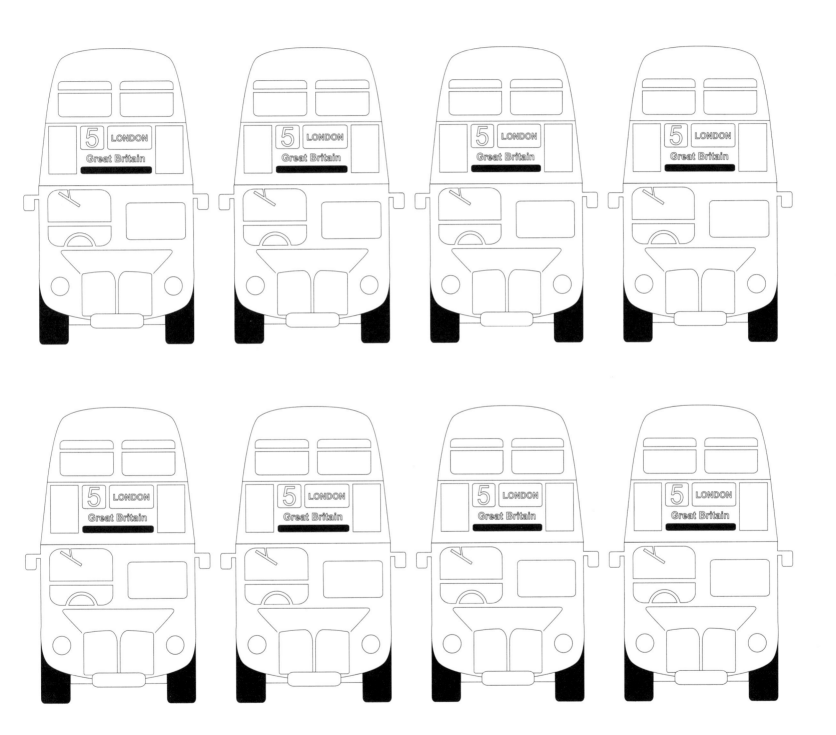

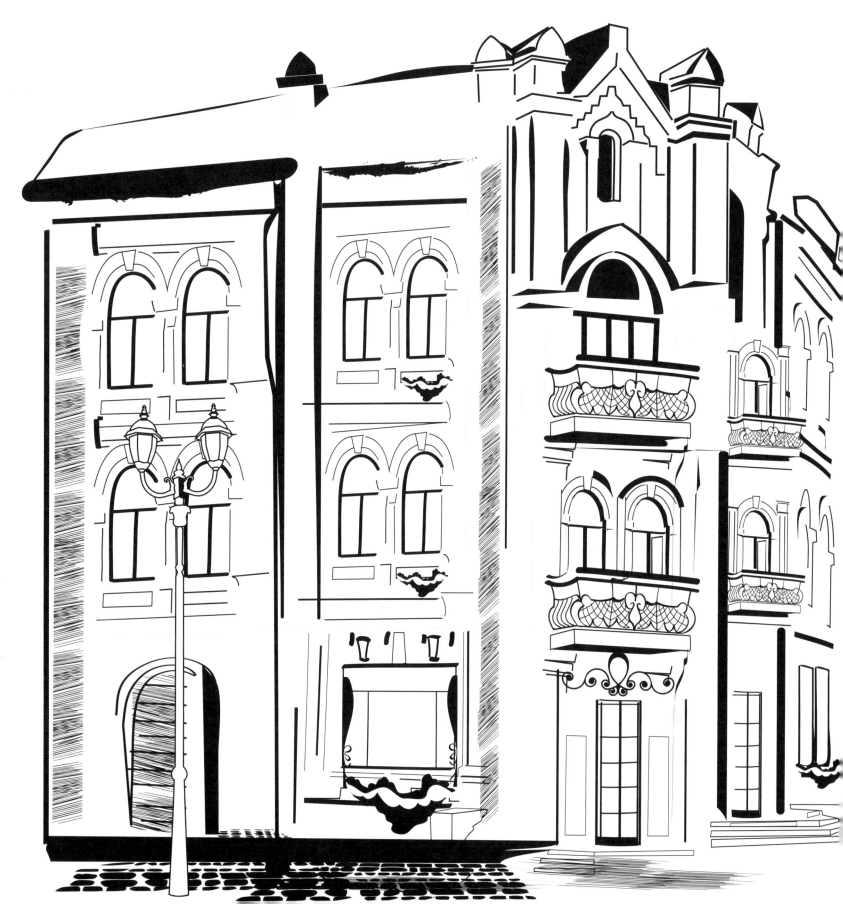

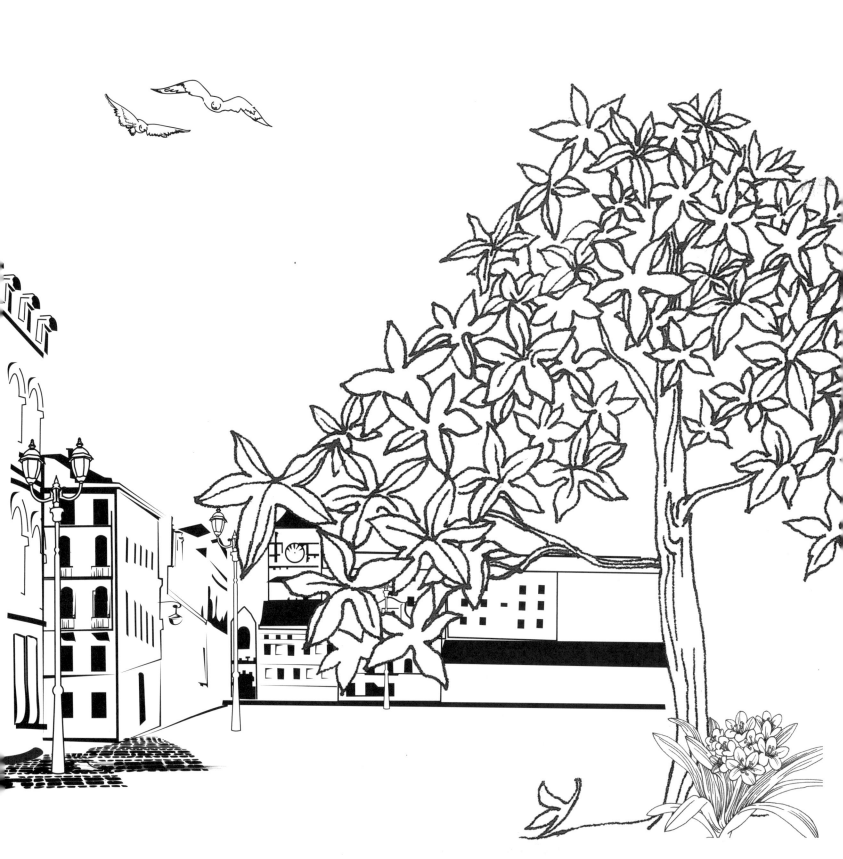

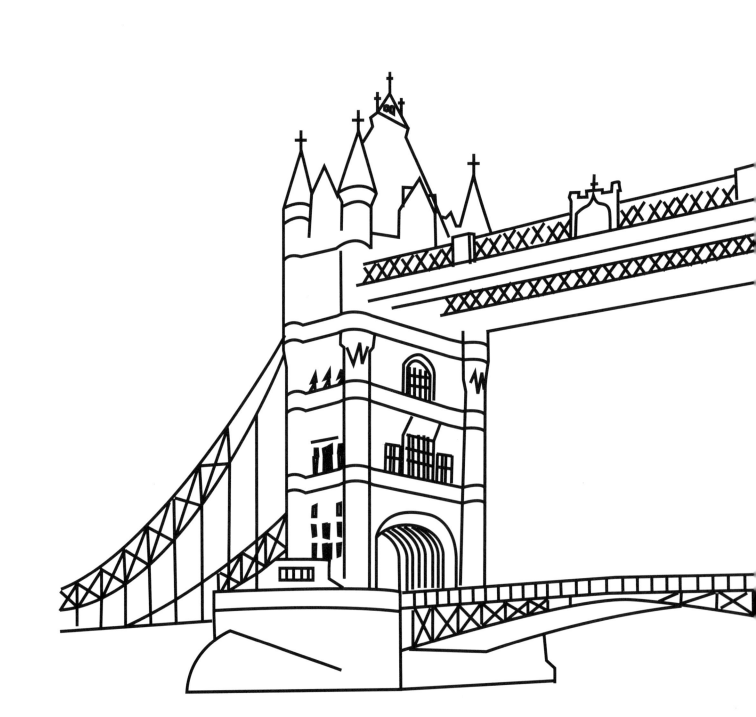

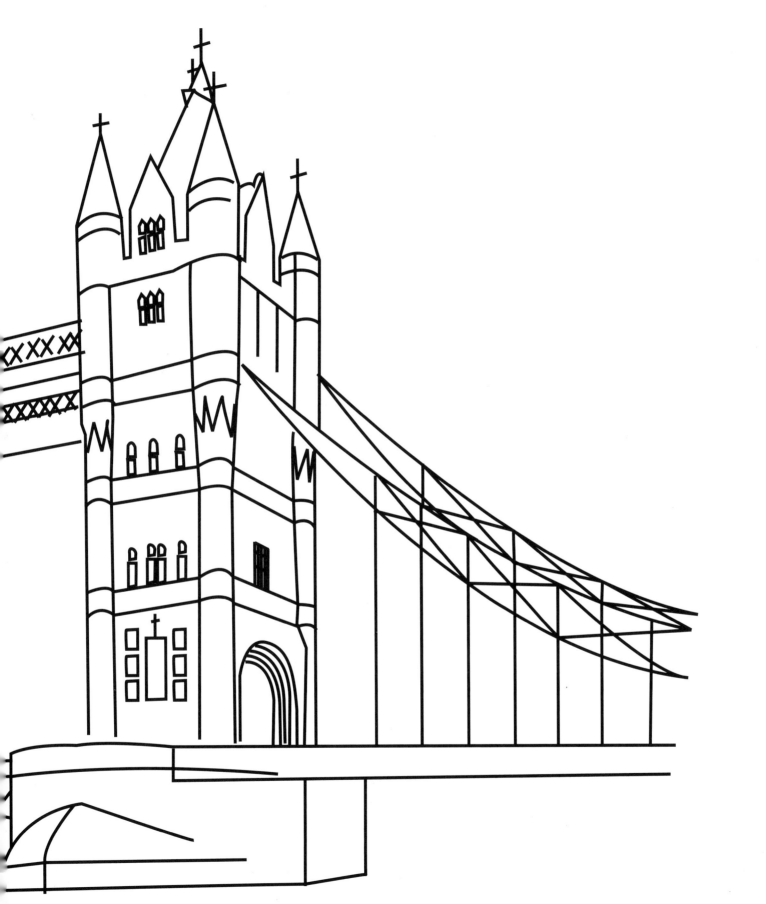

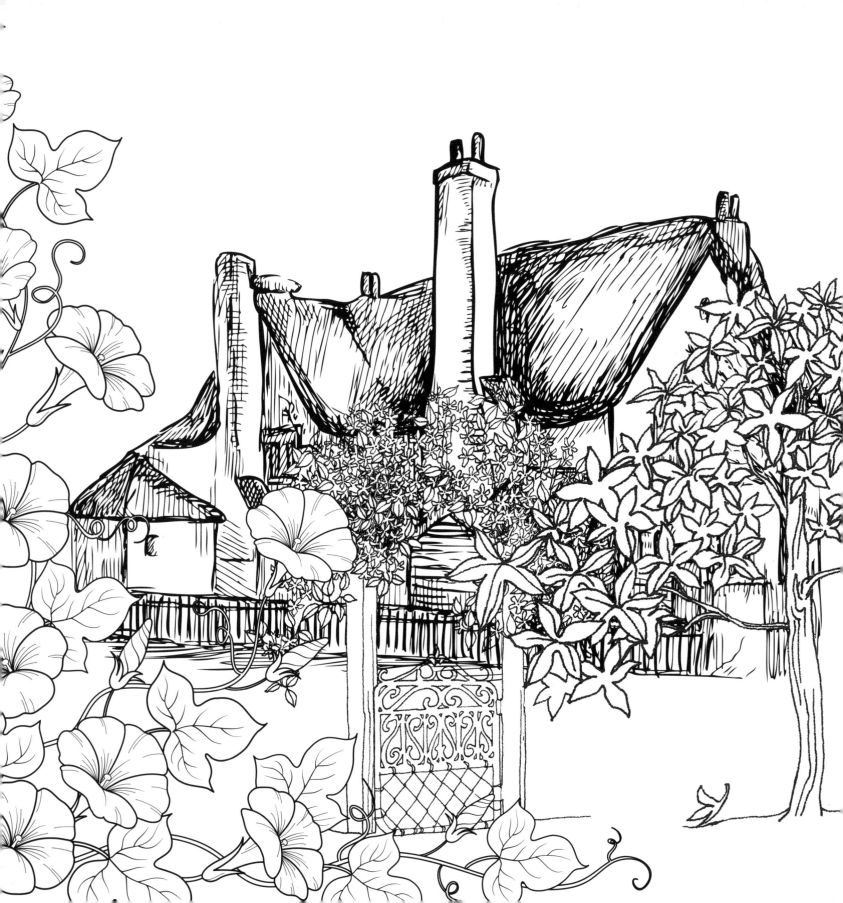

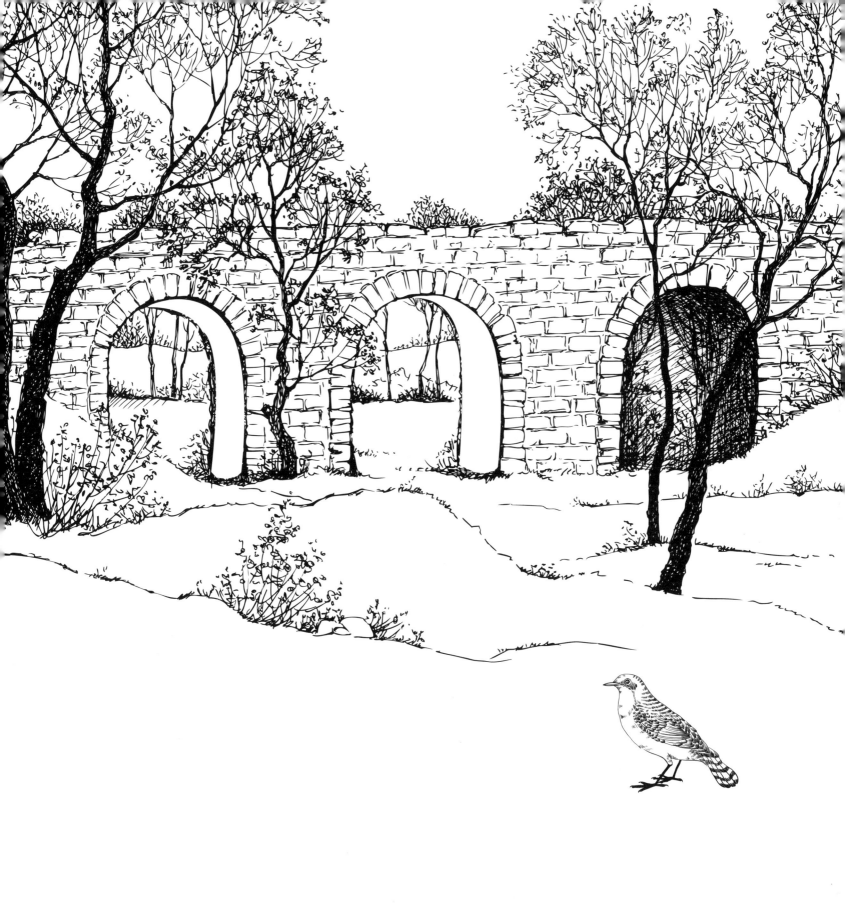

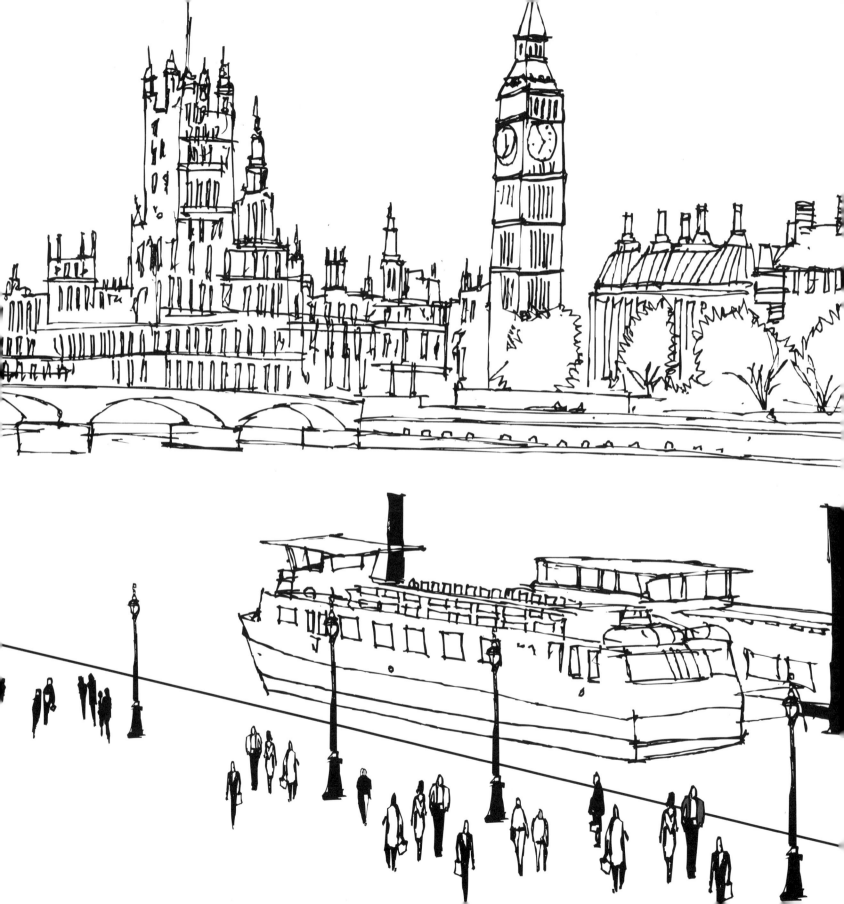

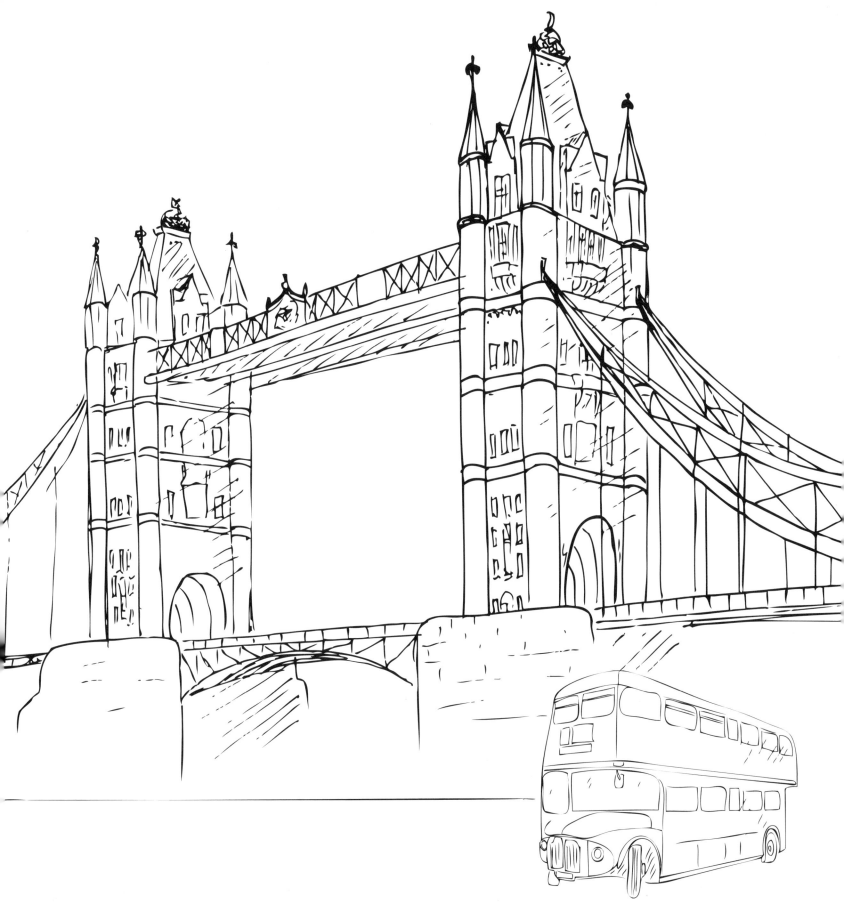

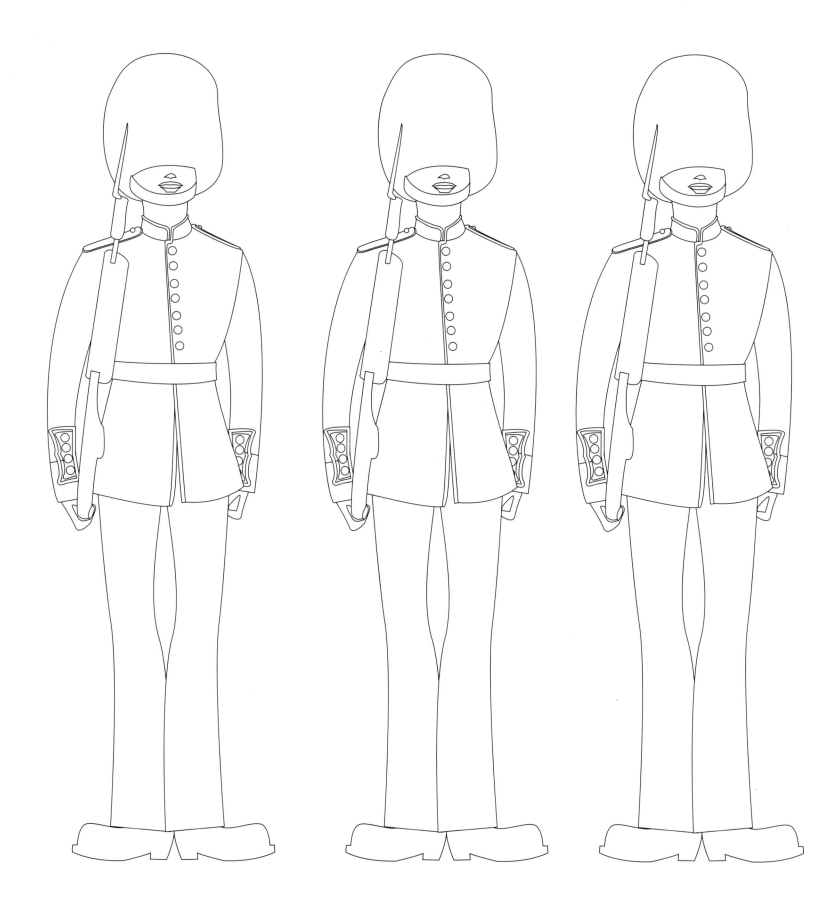

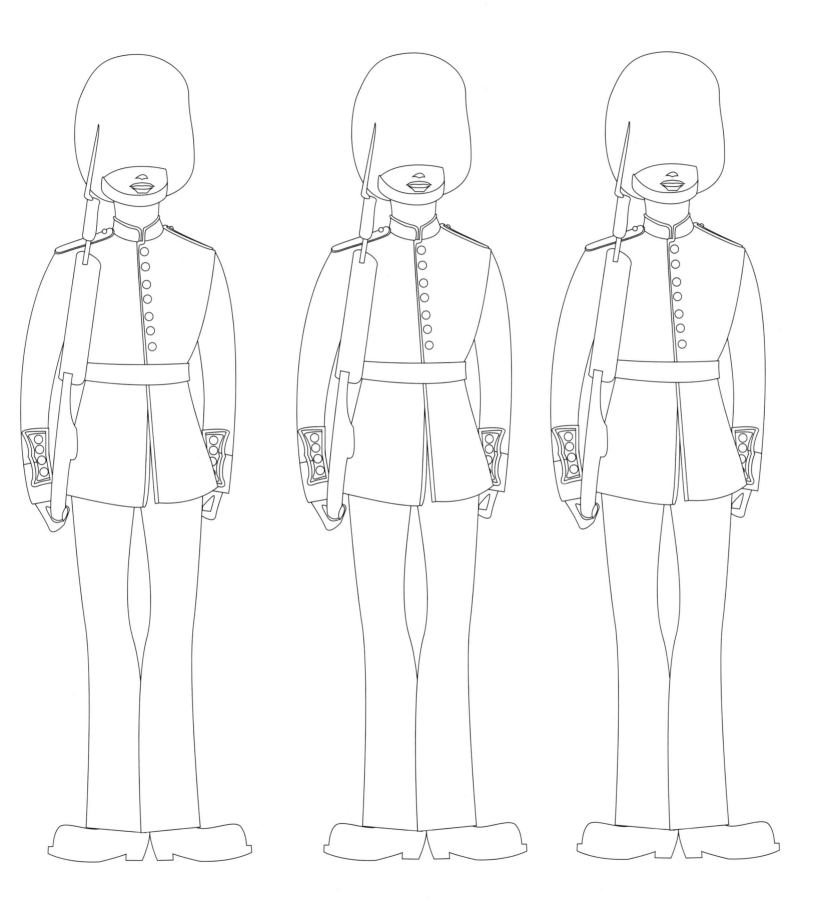

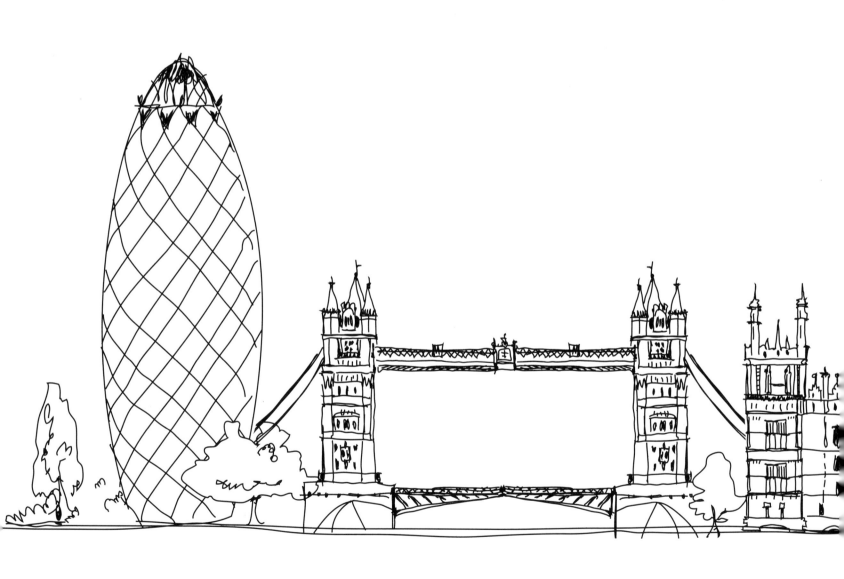

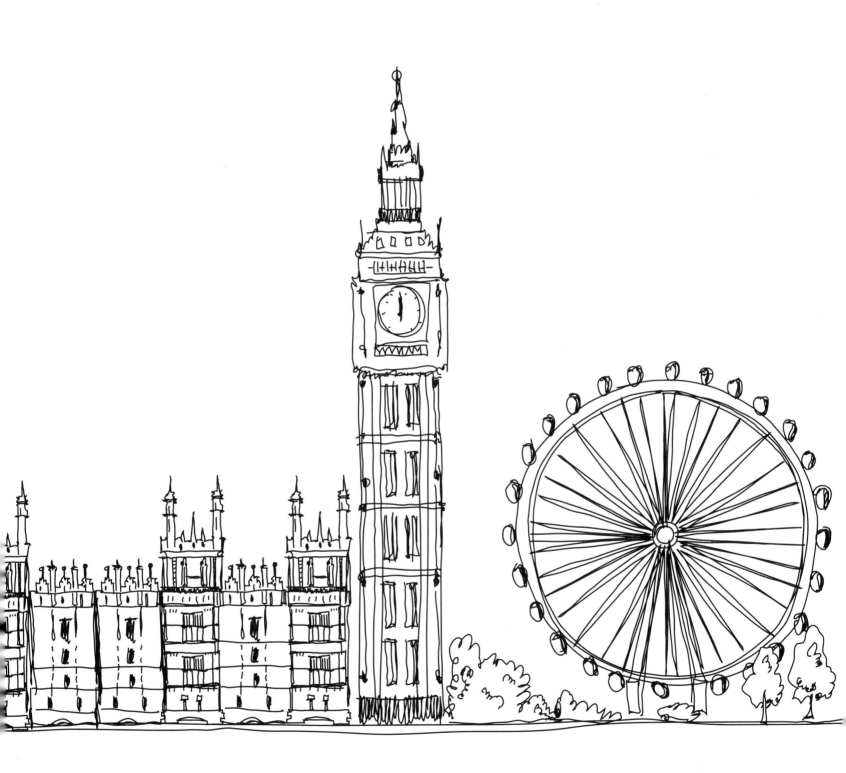

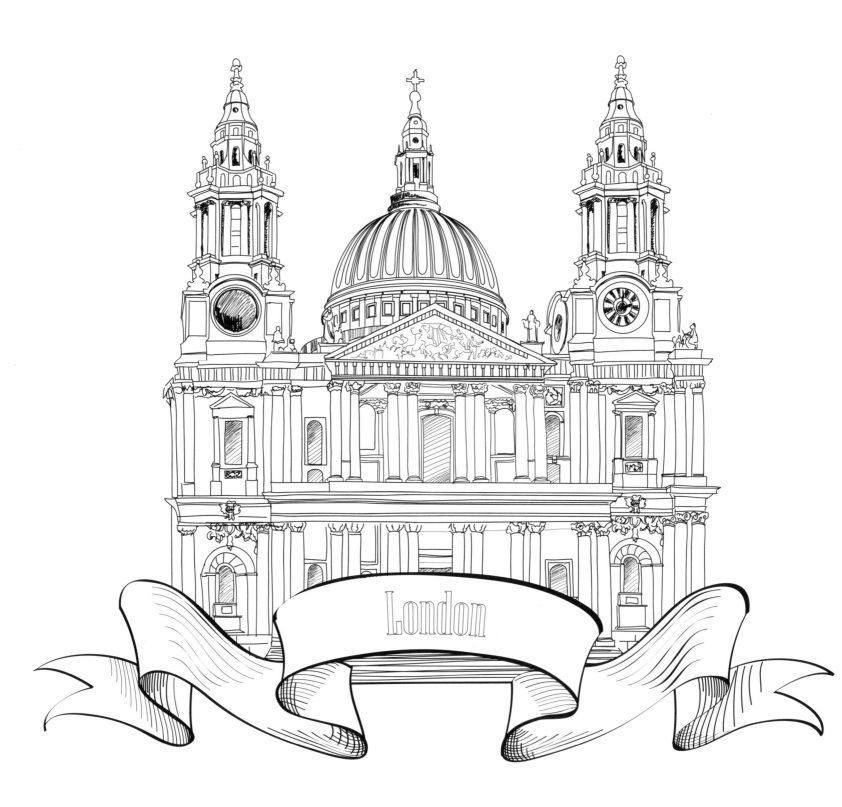
London

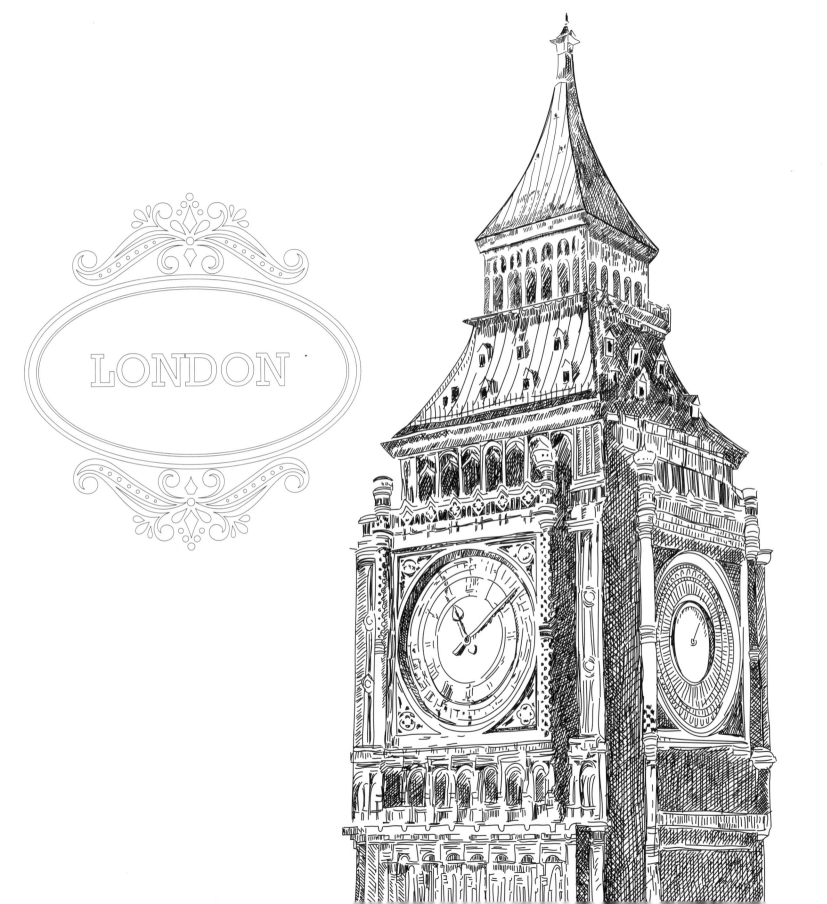

LONDON

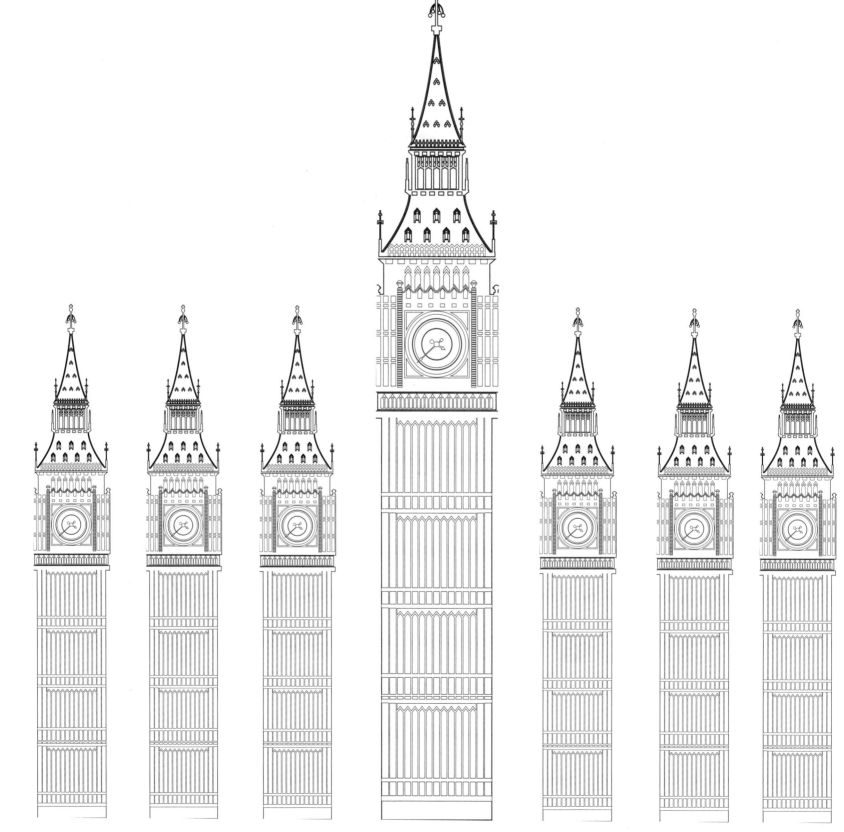

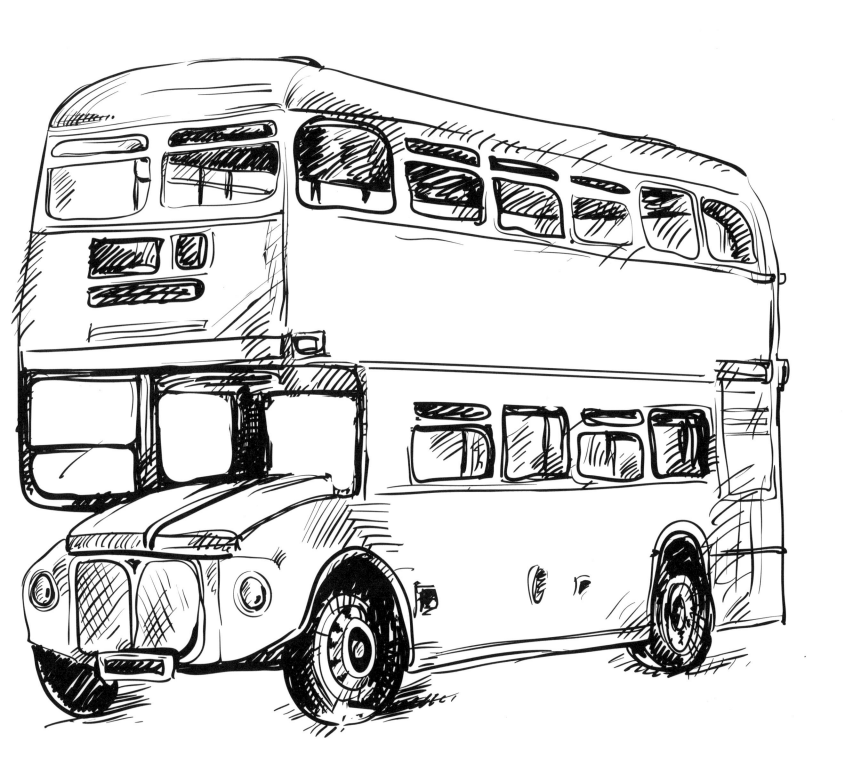

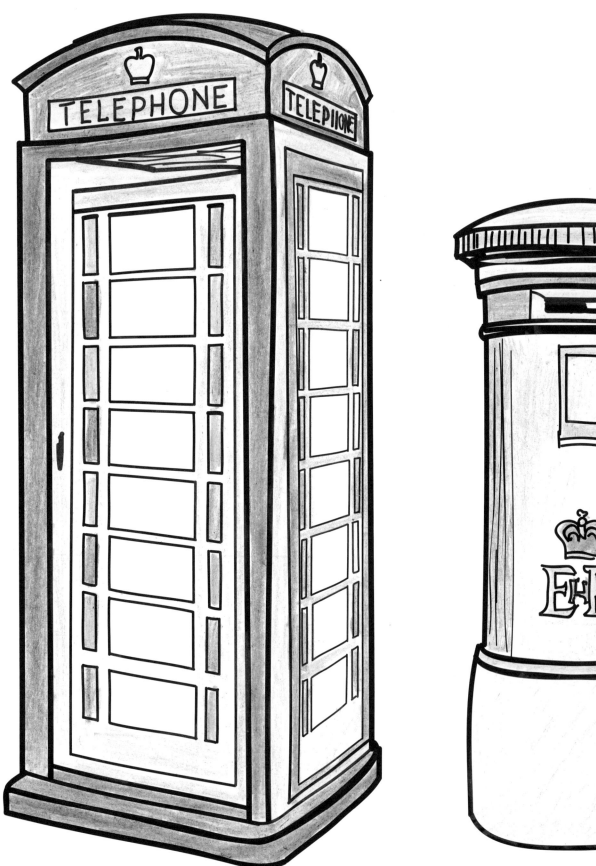

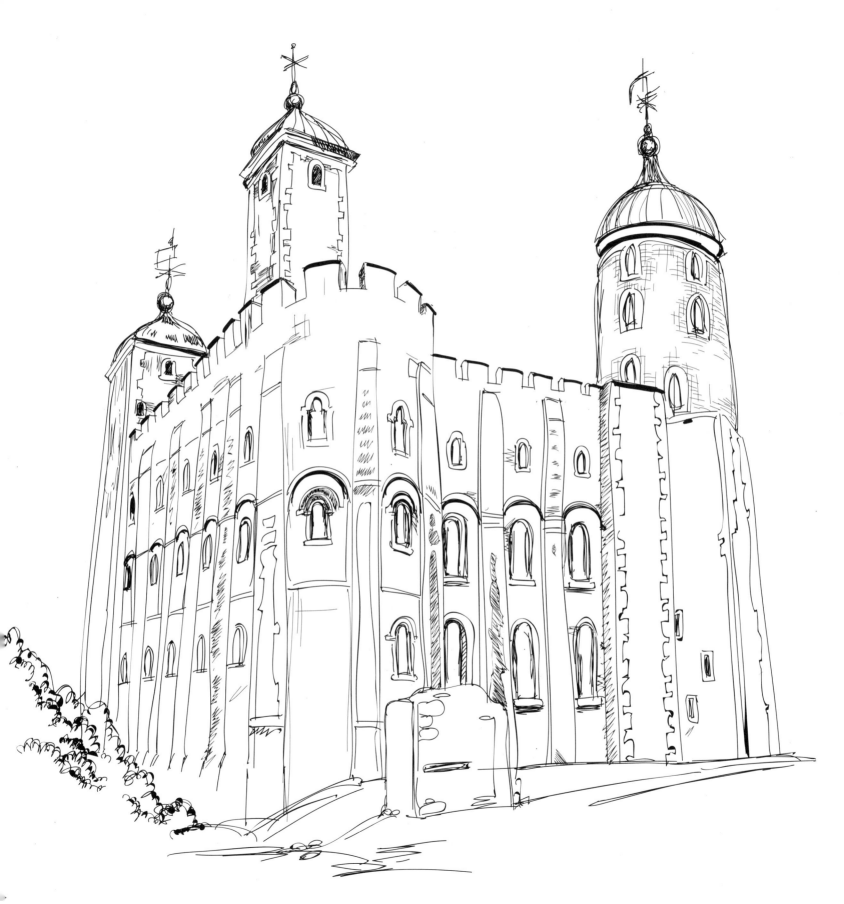

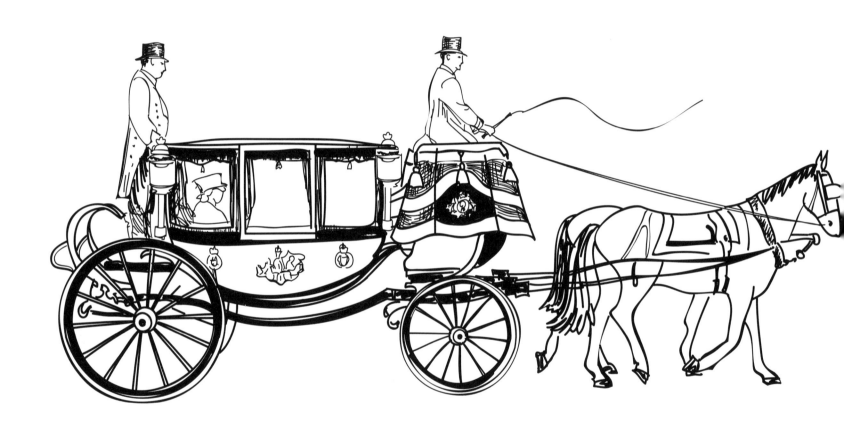

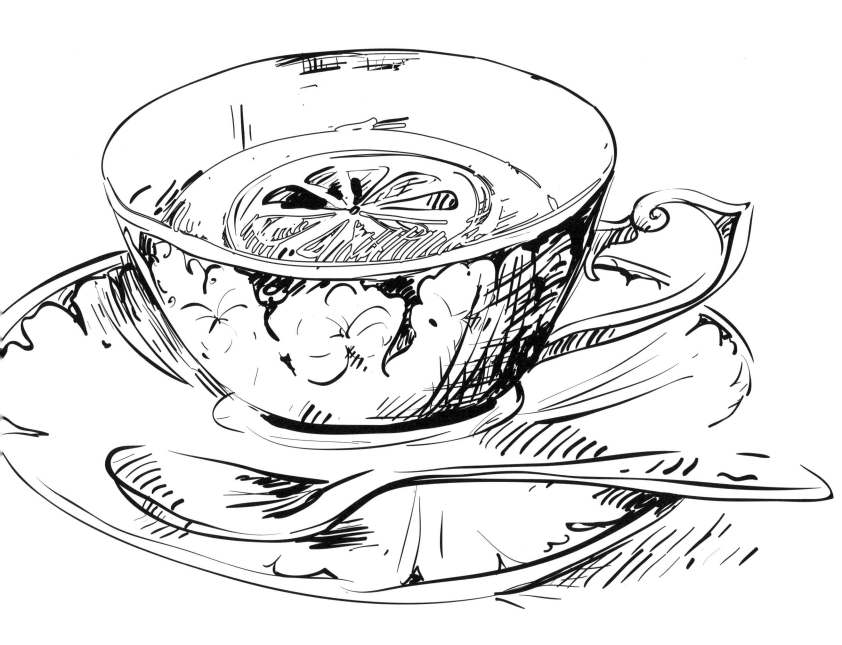

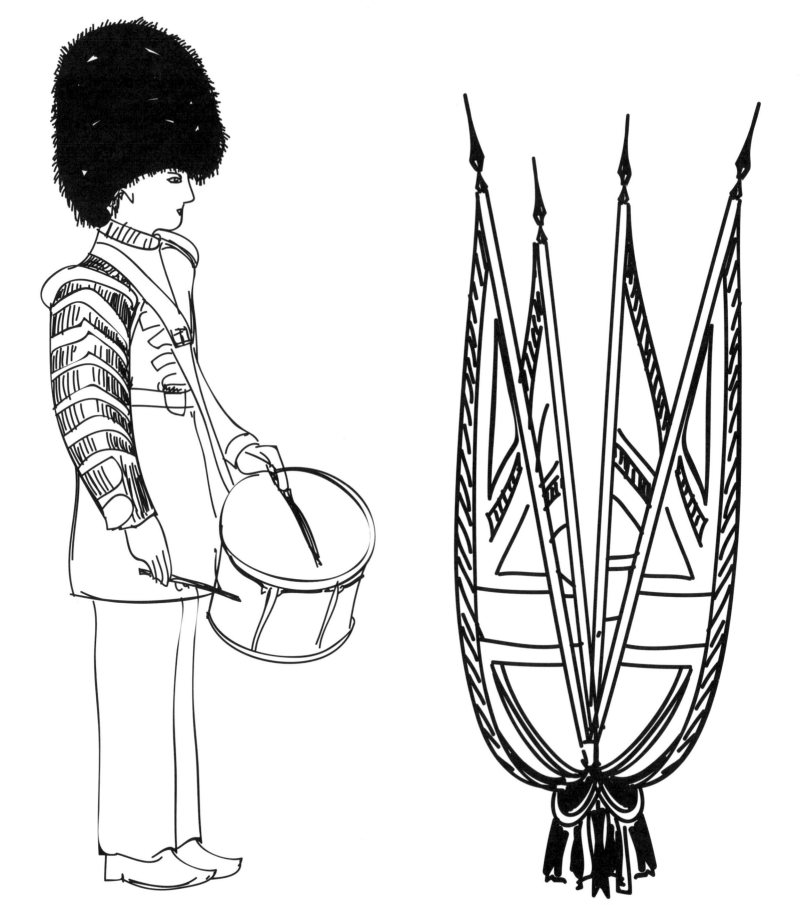

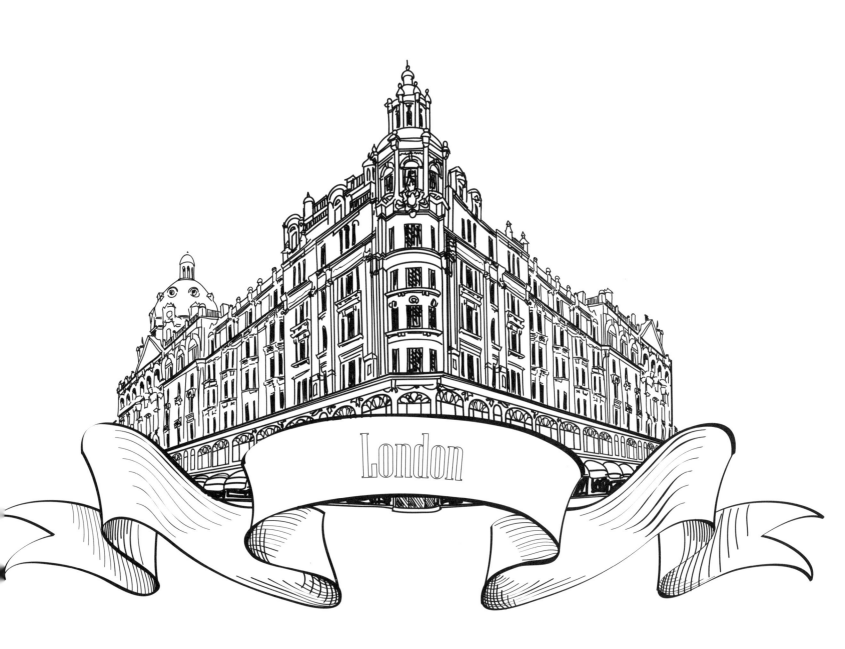

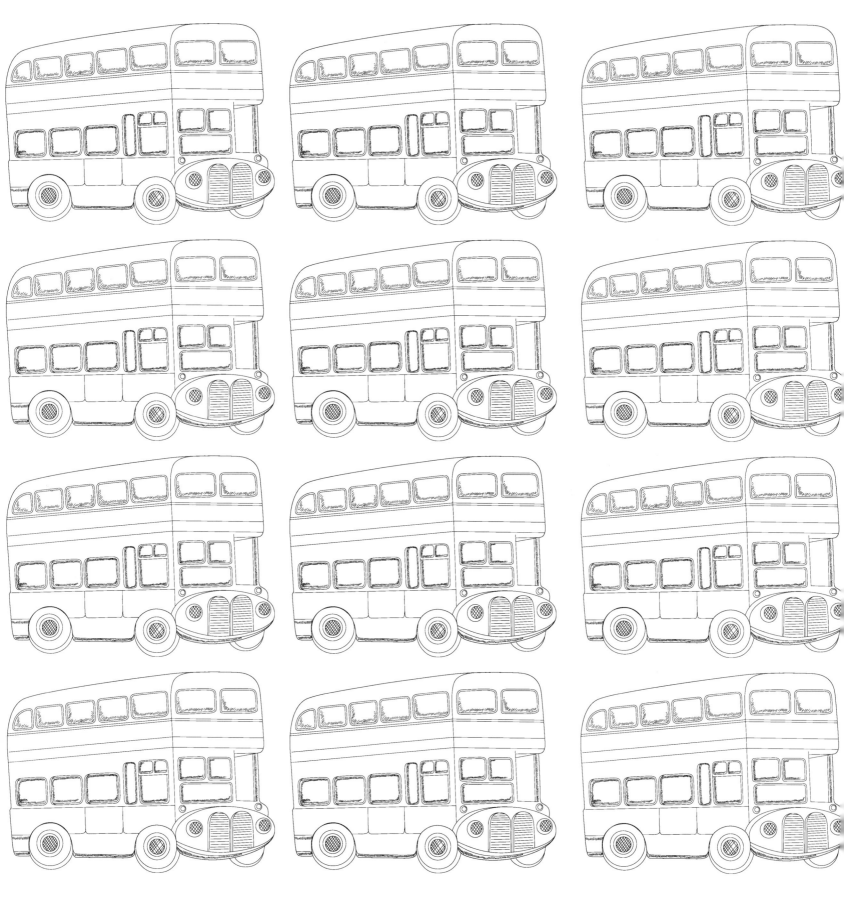

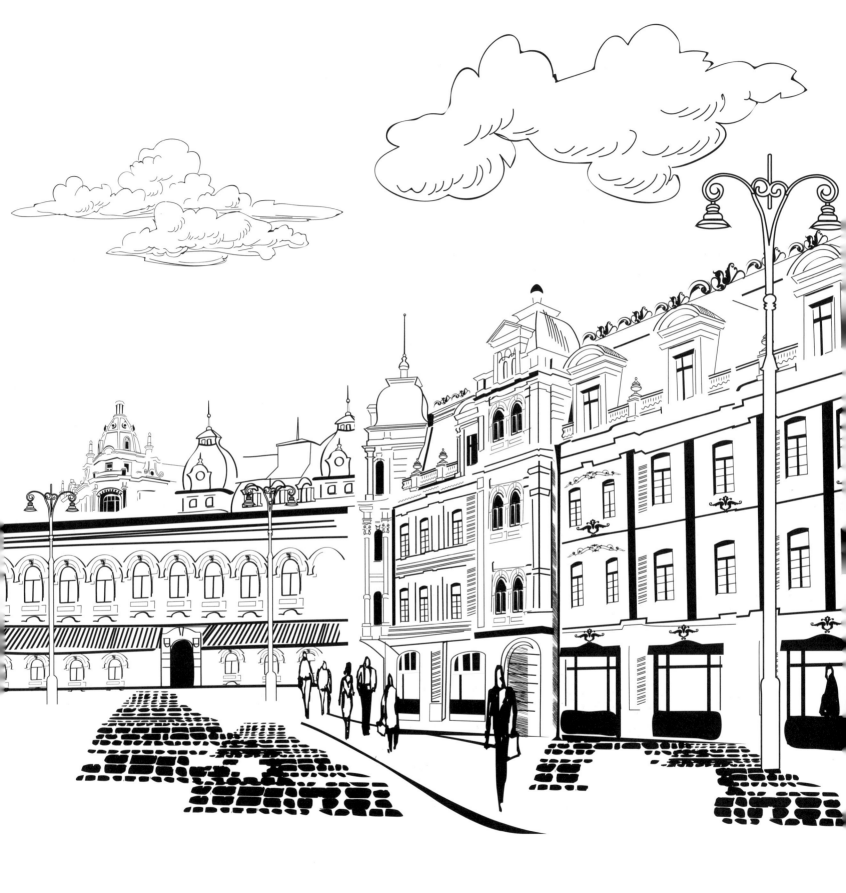

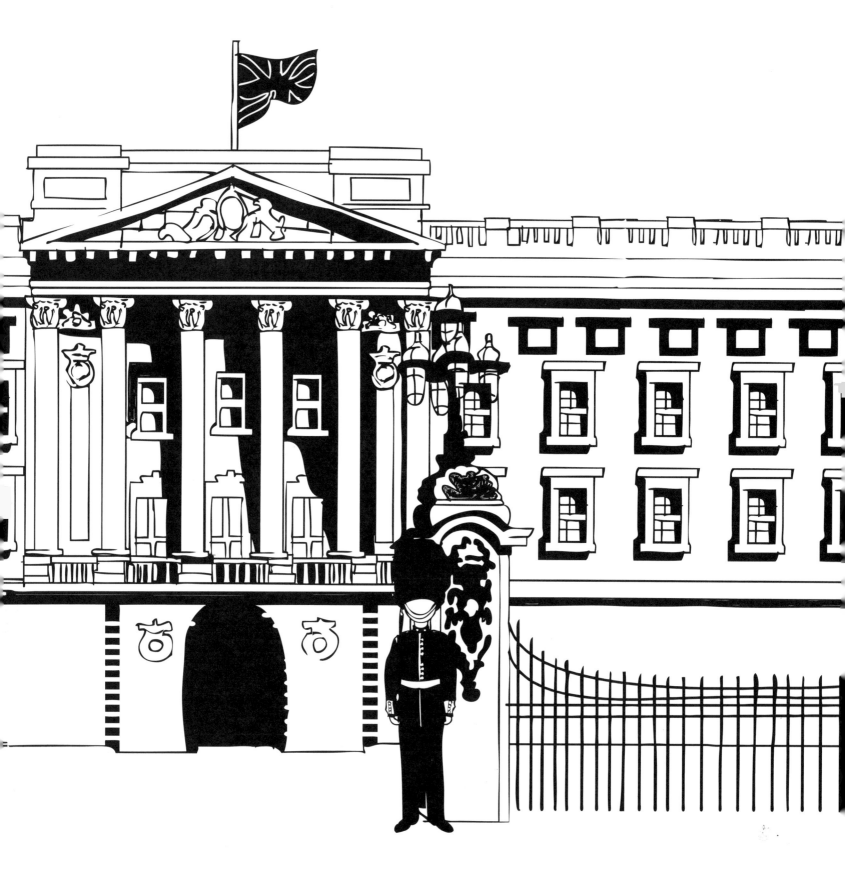

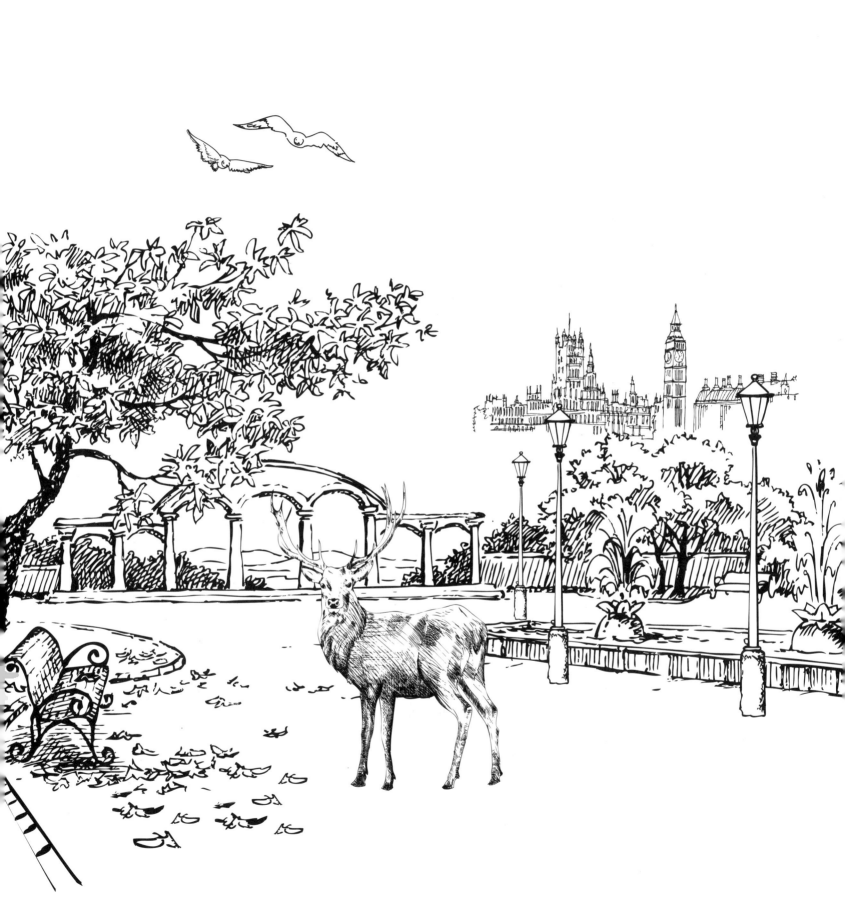

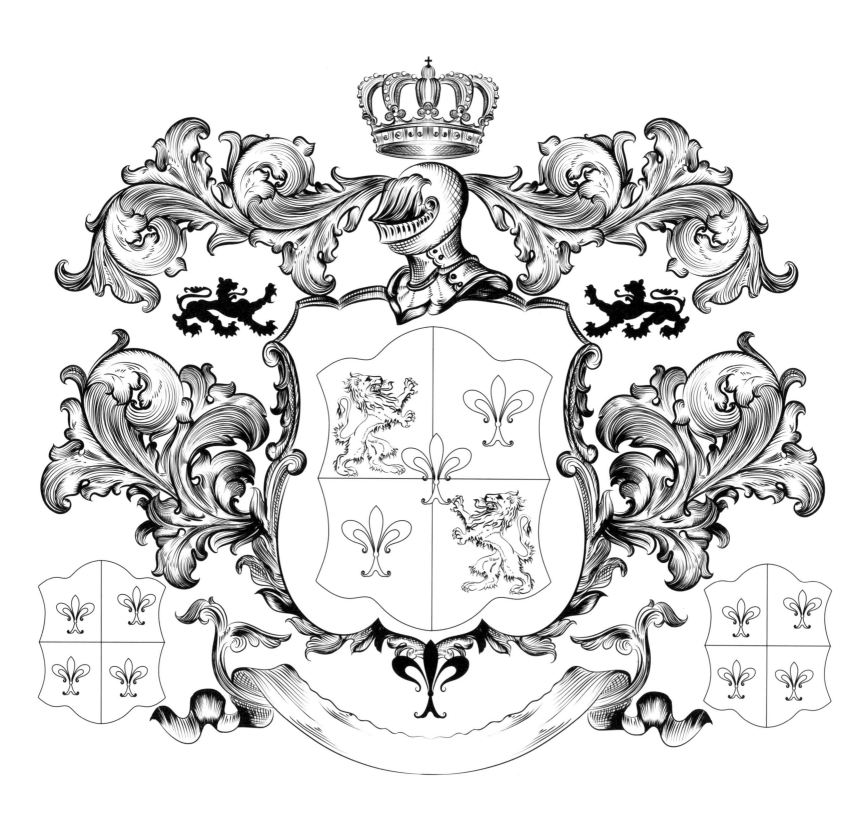

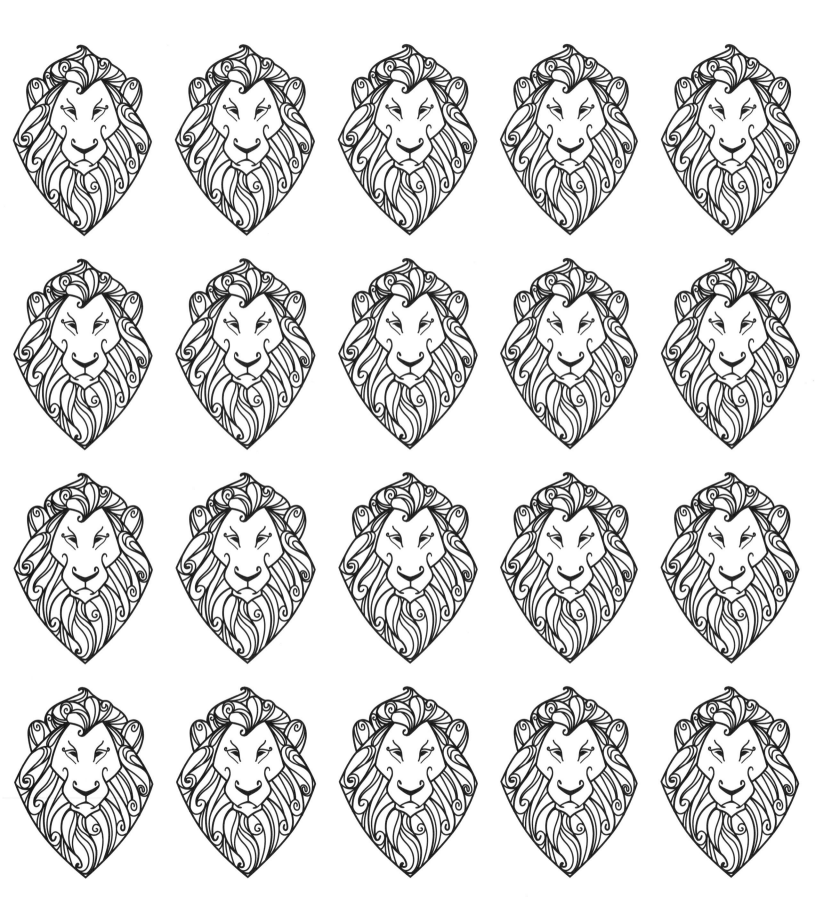

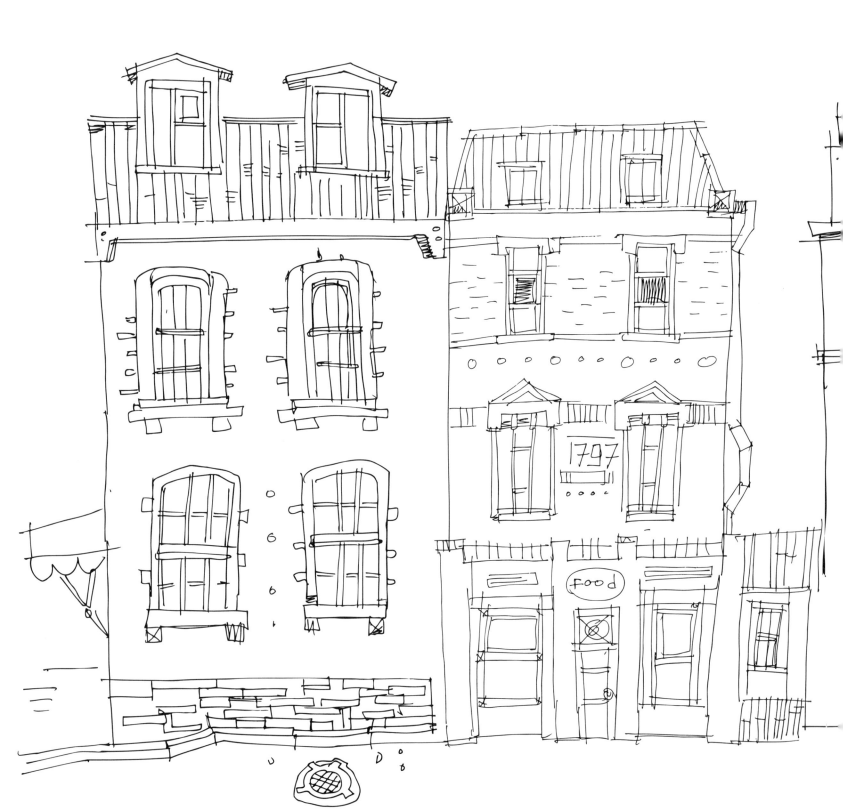

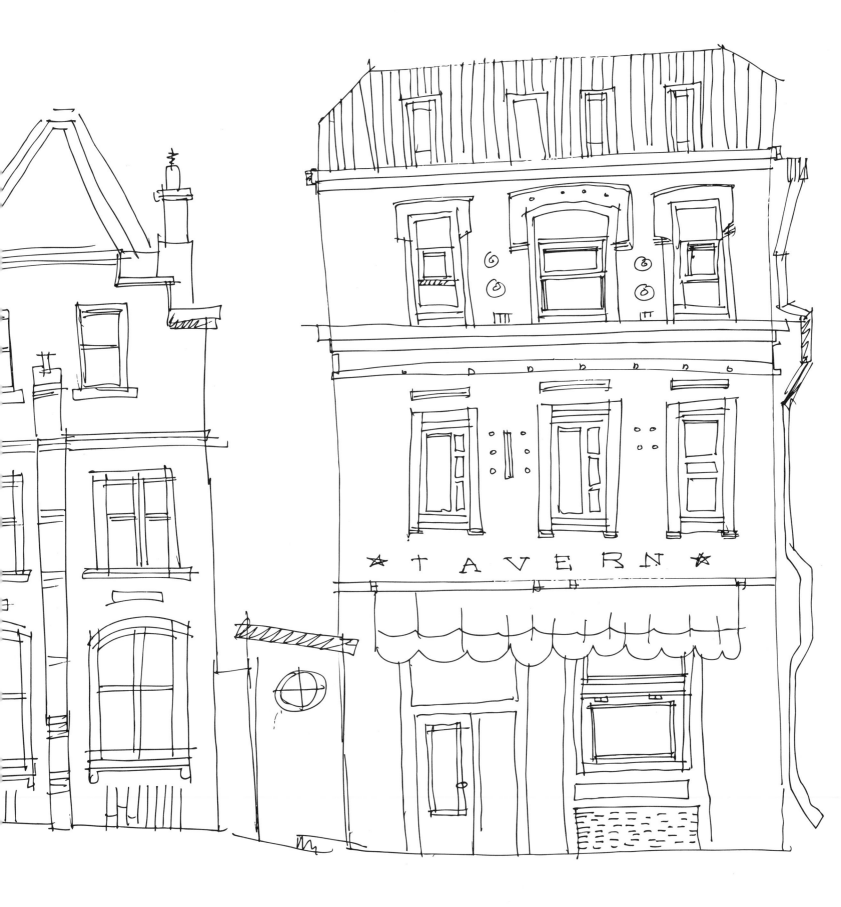

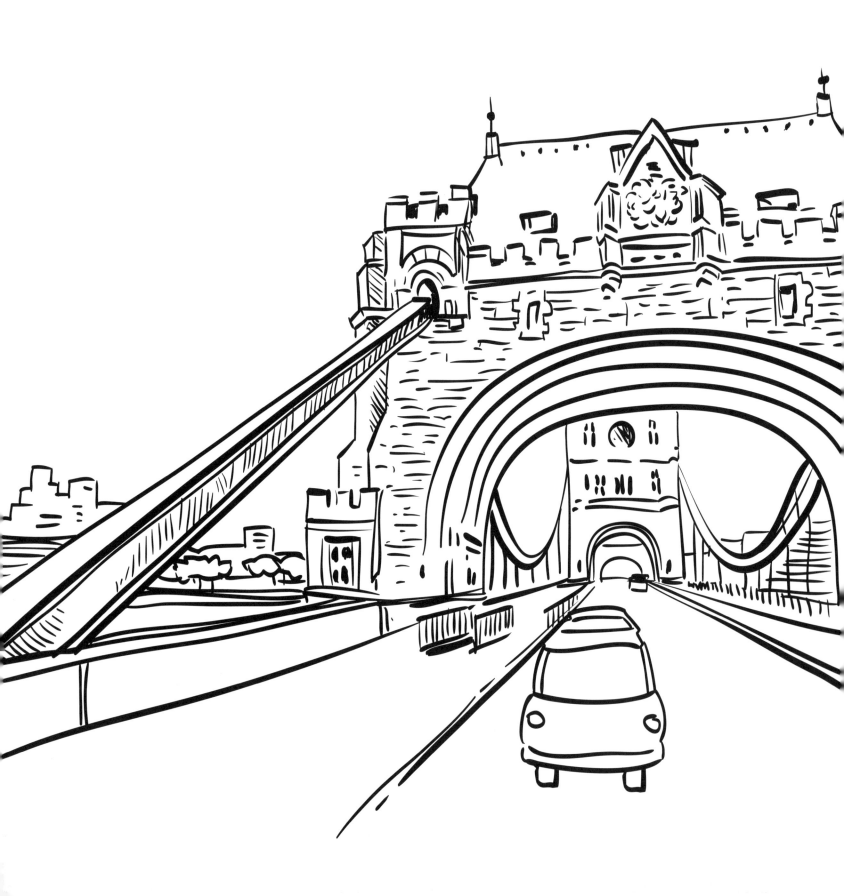

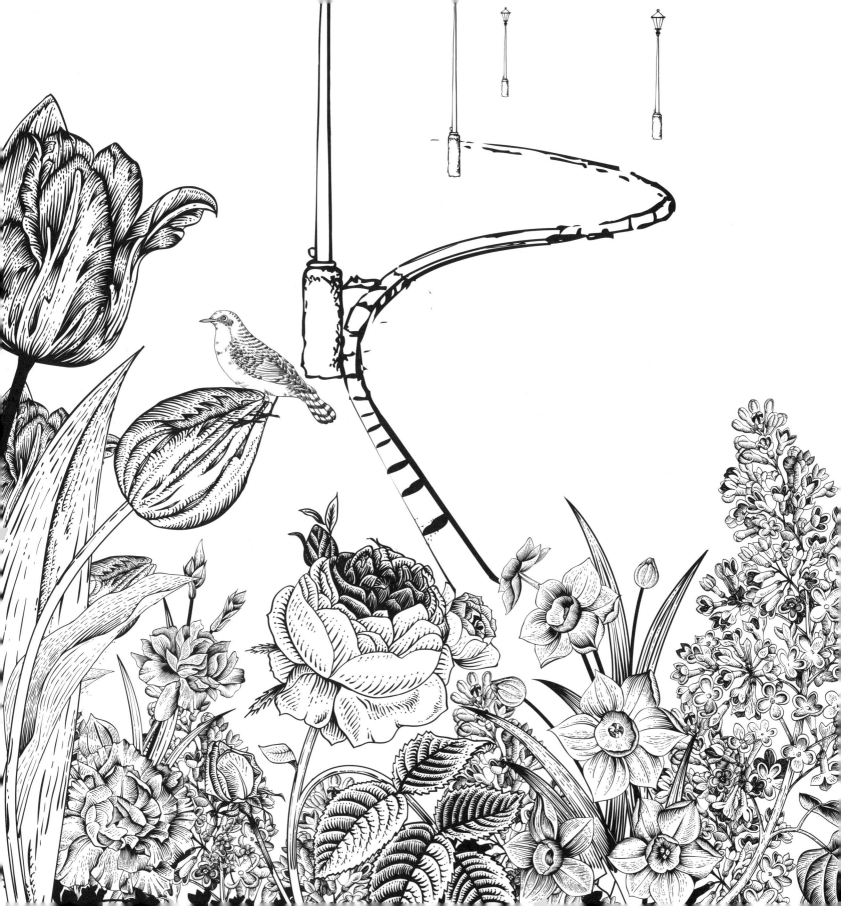

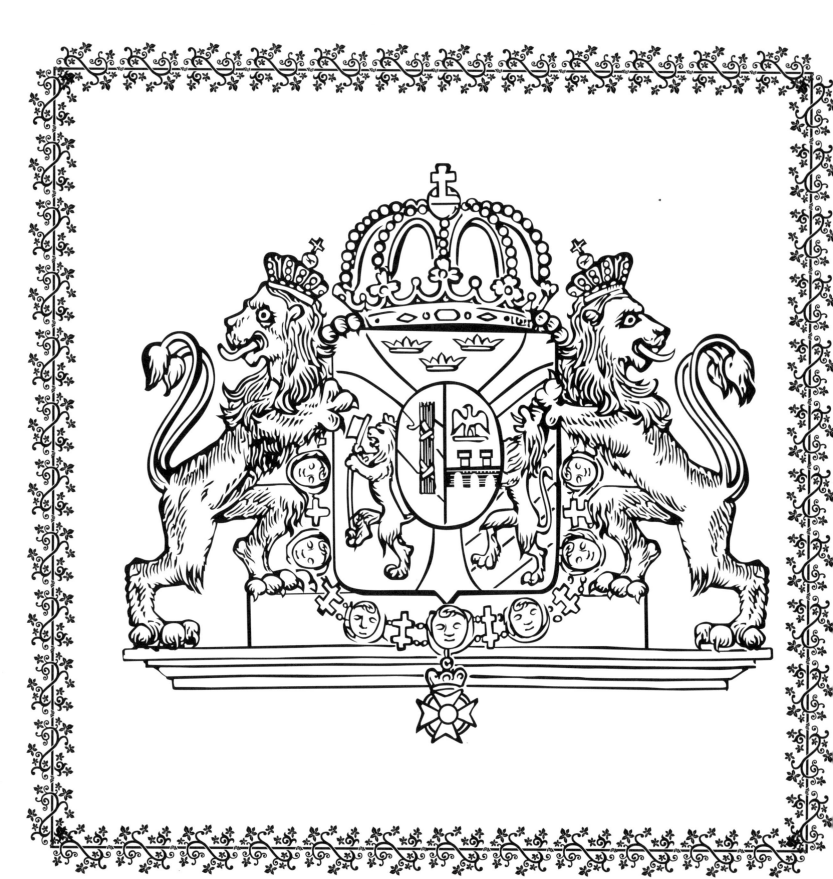

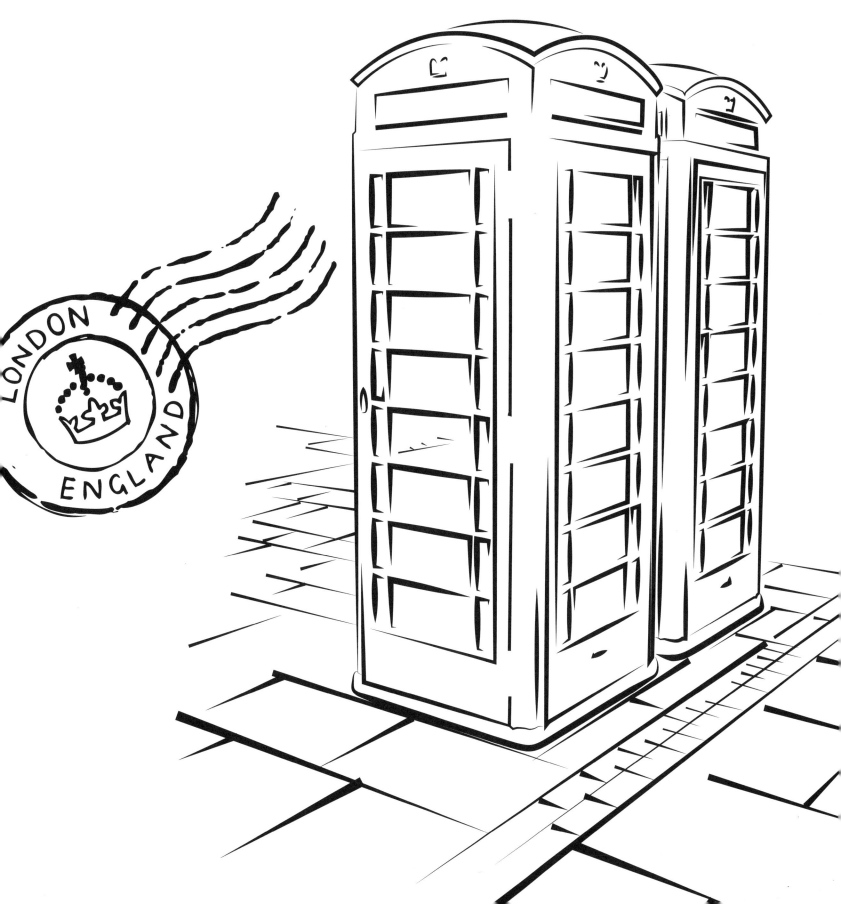

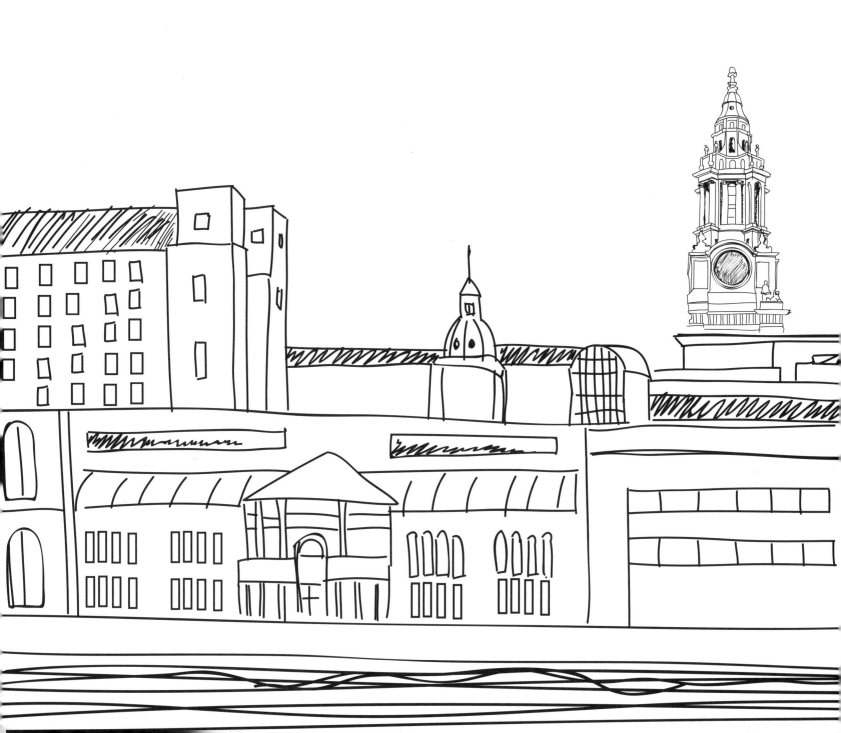

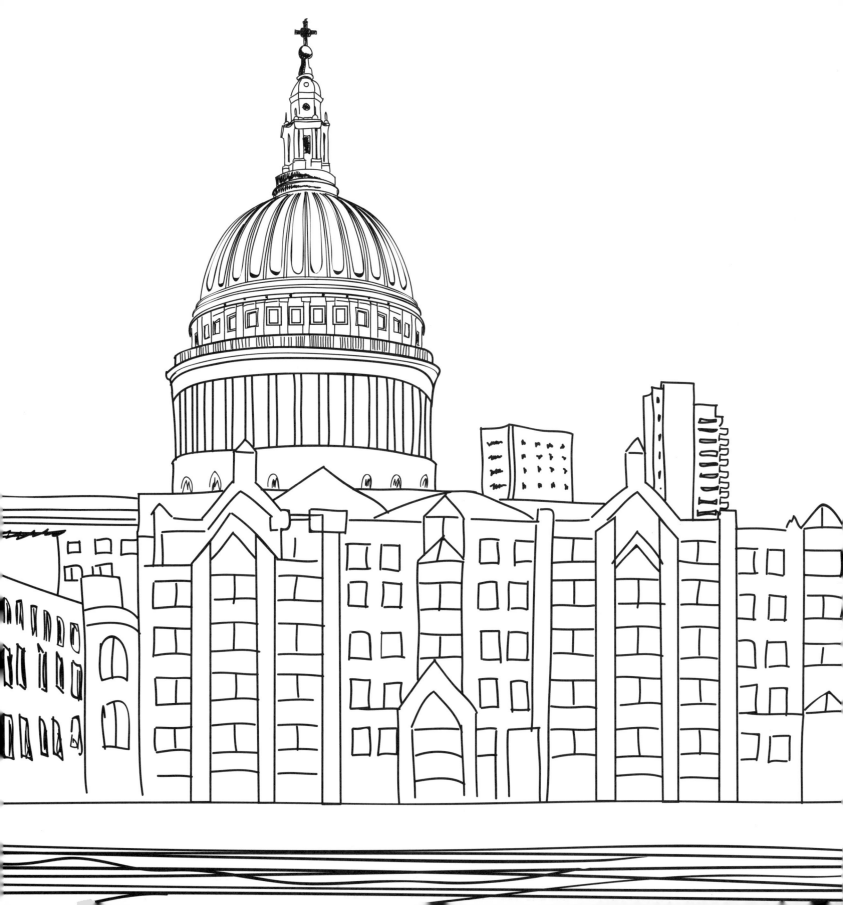

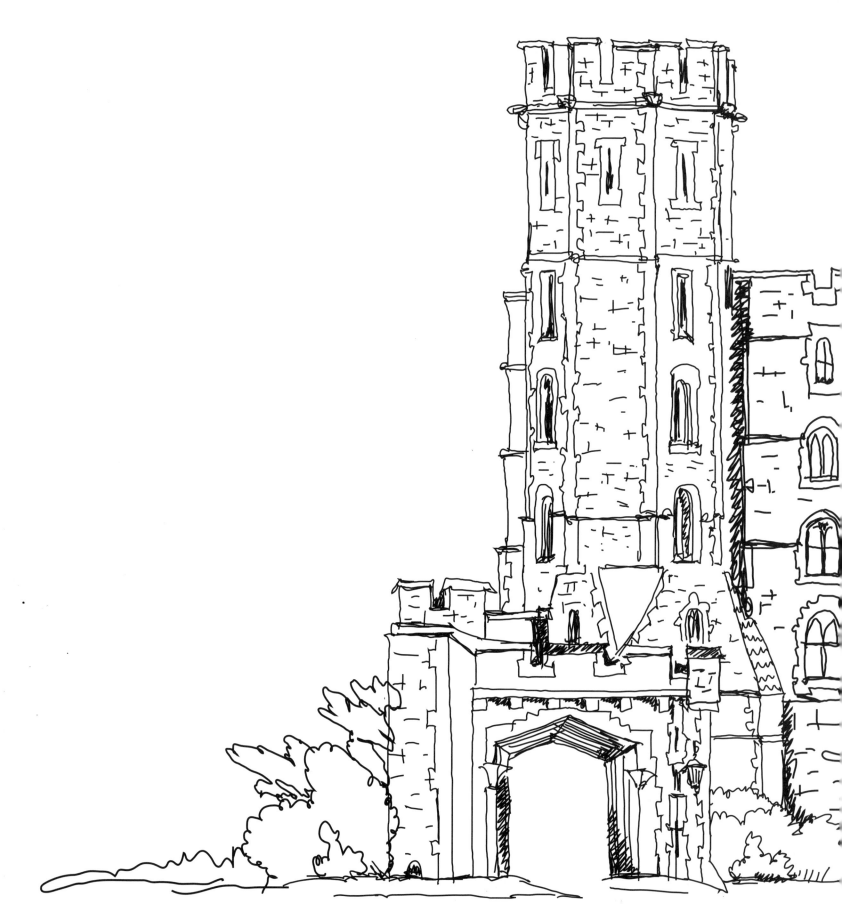

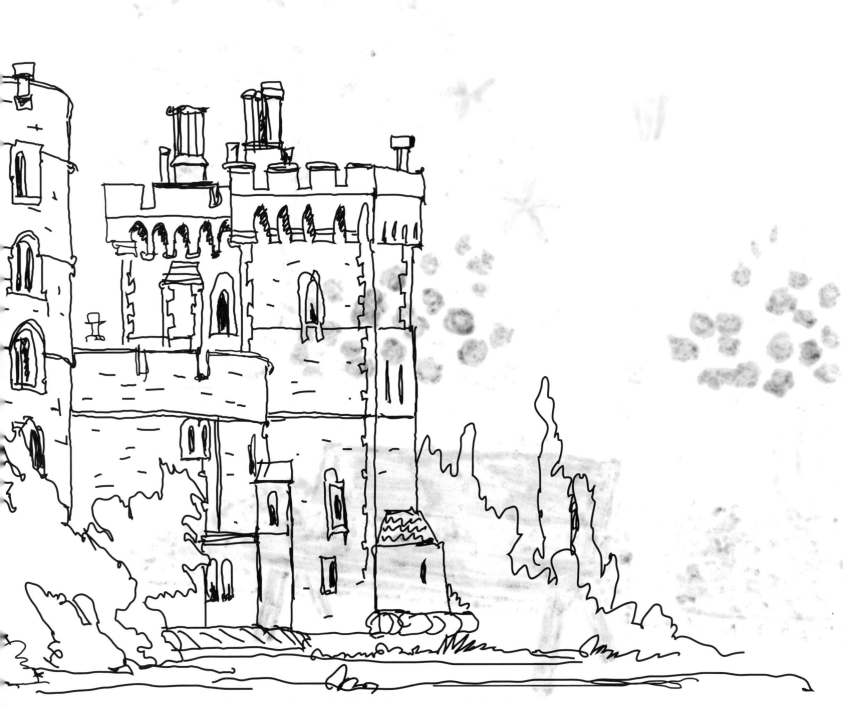

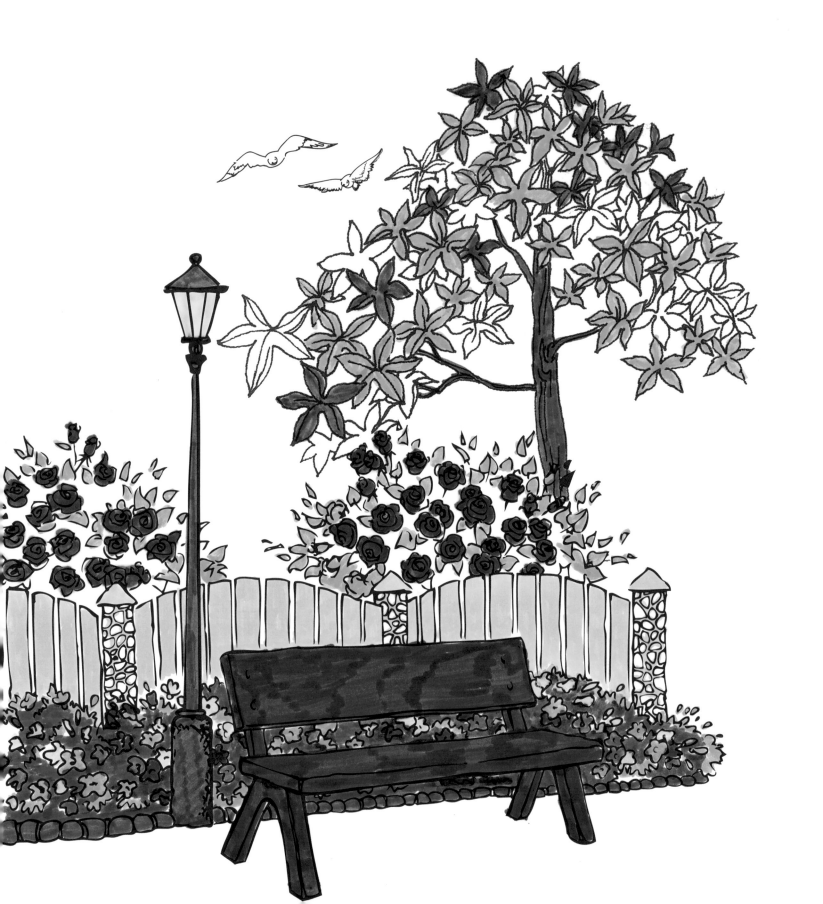

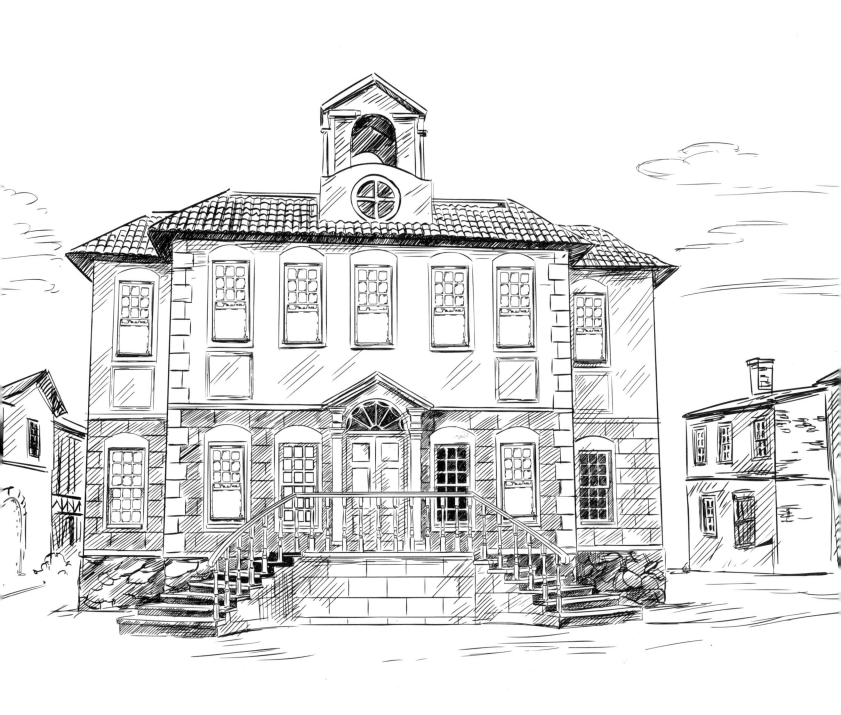

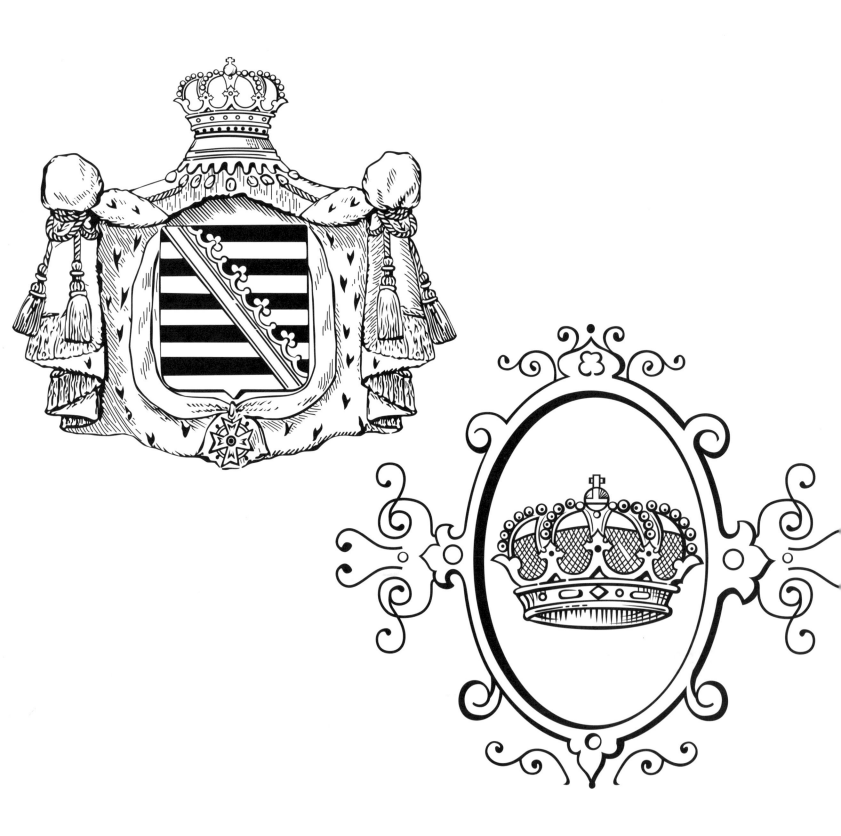

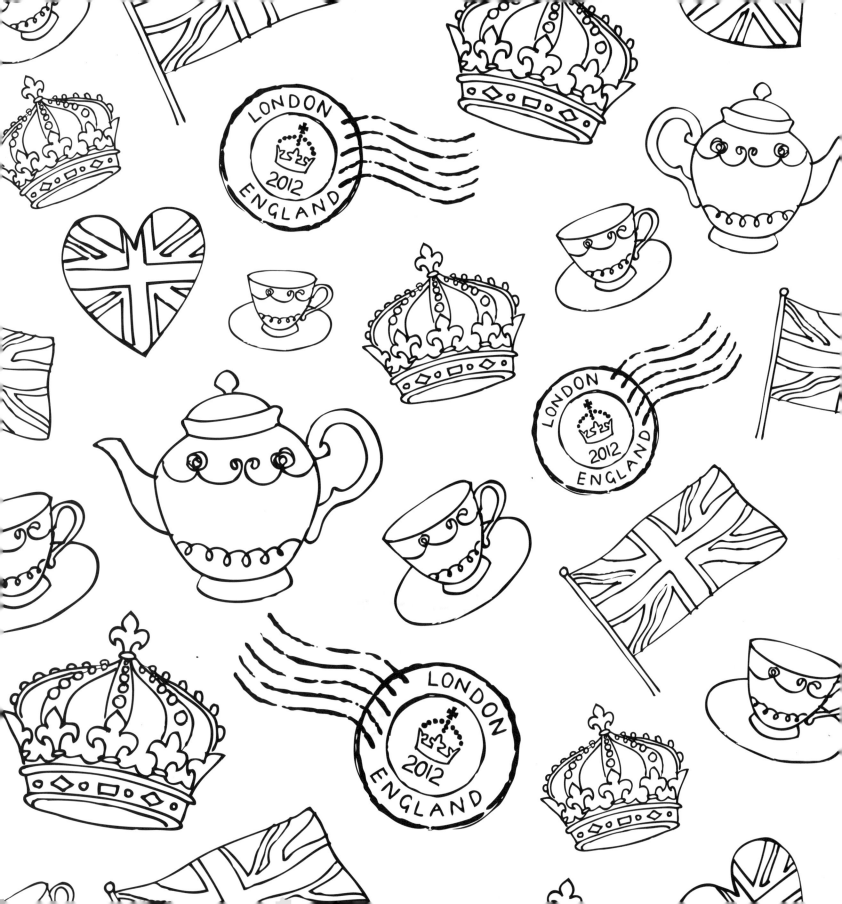

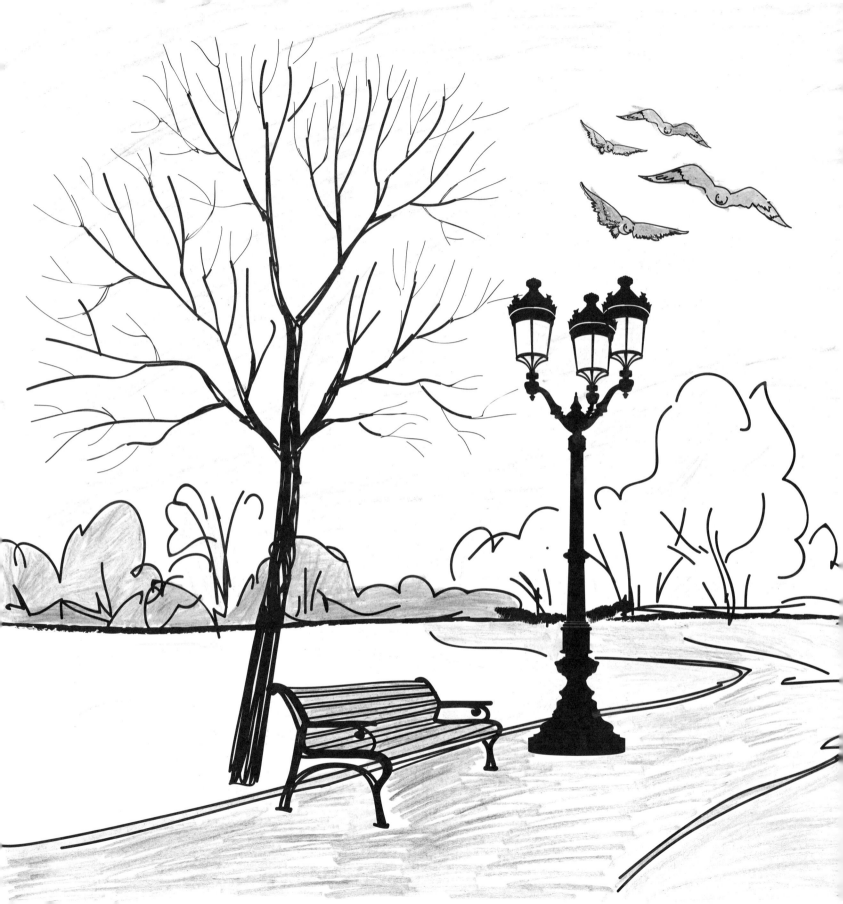

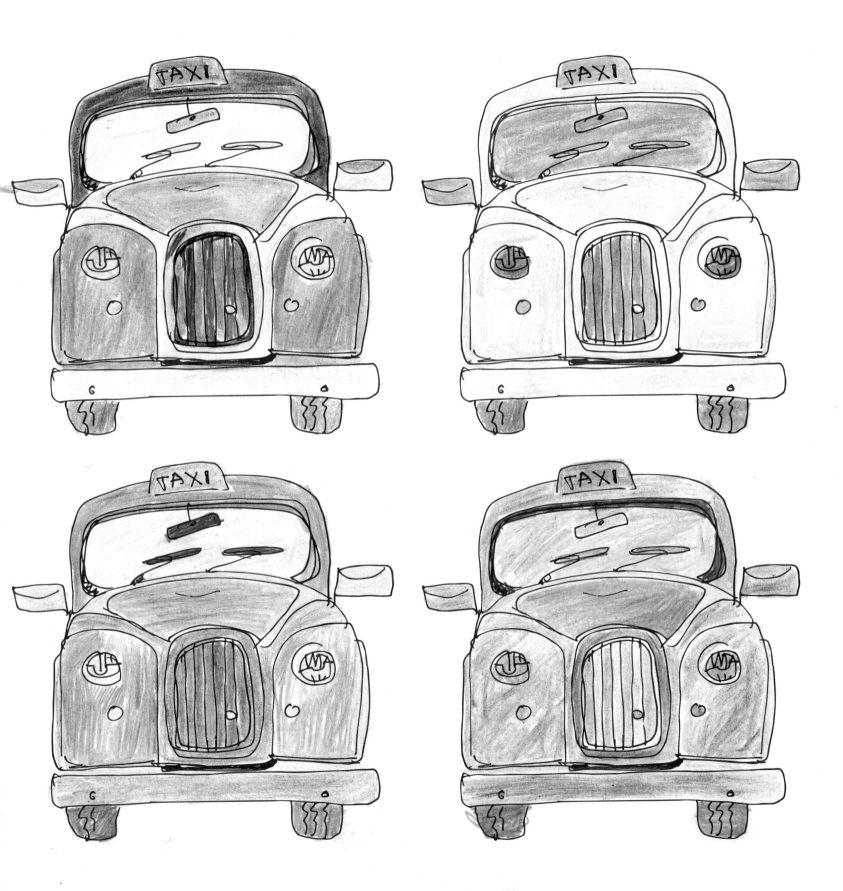

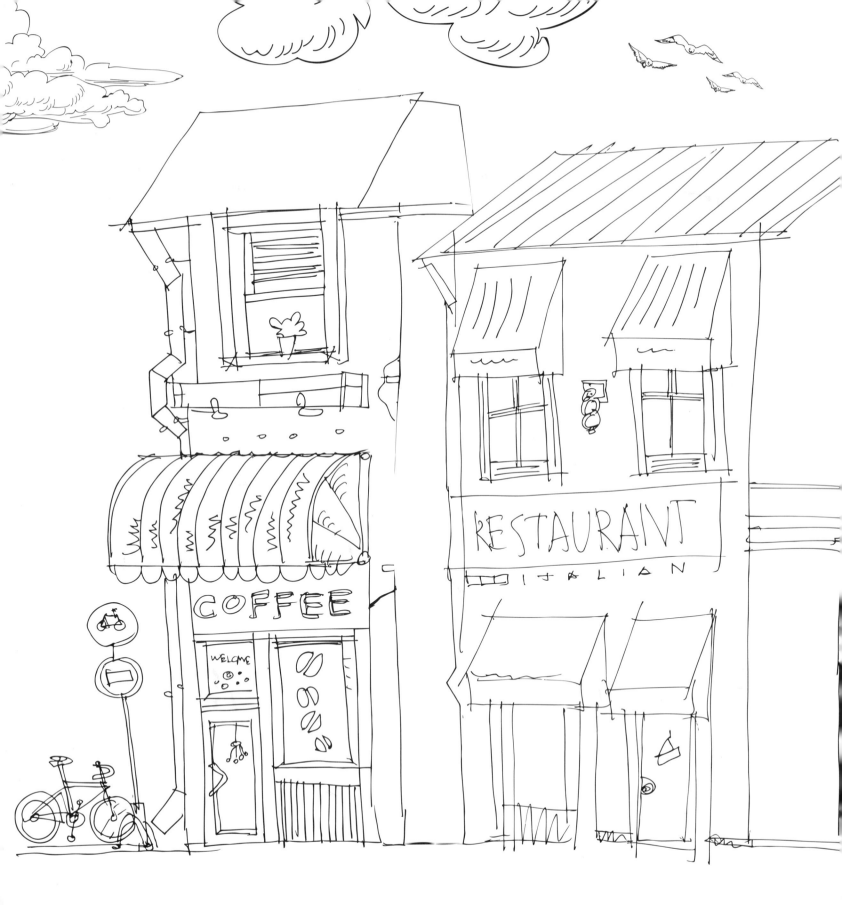

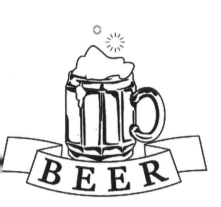

BEER

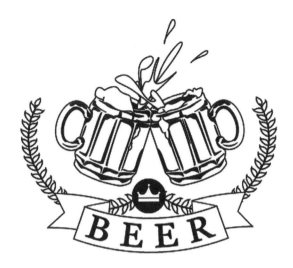

BEER

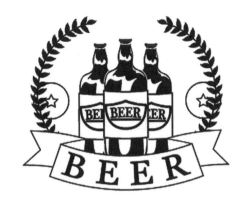

BEER

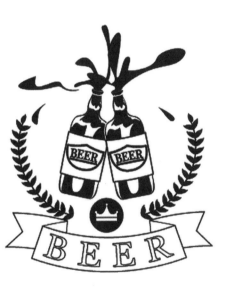

BEER

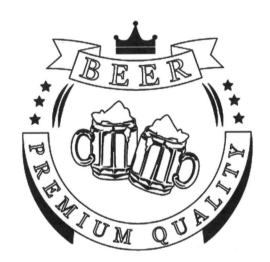

BEER

PREMIUM QUALITY

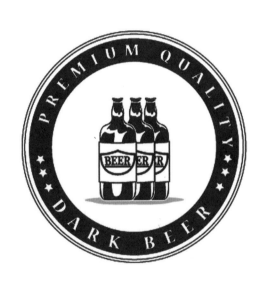

PREMIUM QUALITY

DARK BEER

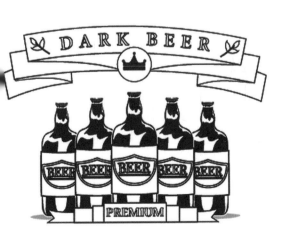

DARK BEER

BEER

PREMIUM

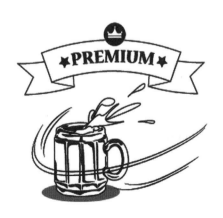

PREMIUM

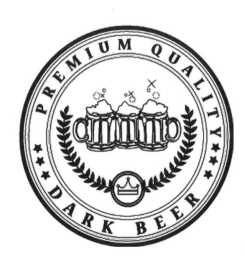

PREMIUM QUALITY

DARK BEER

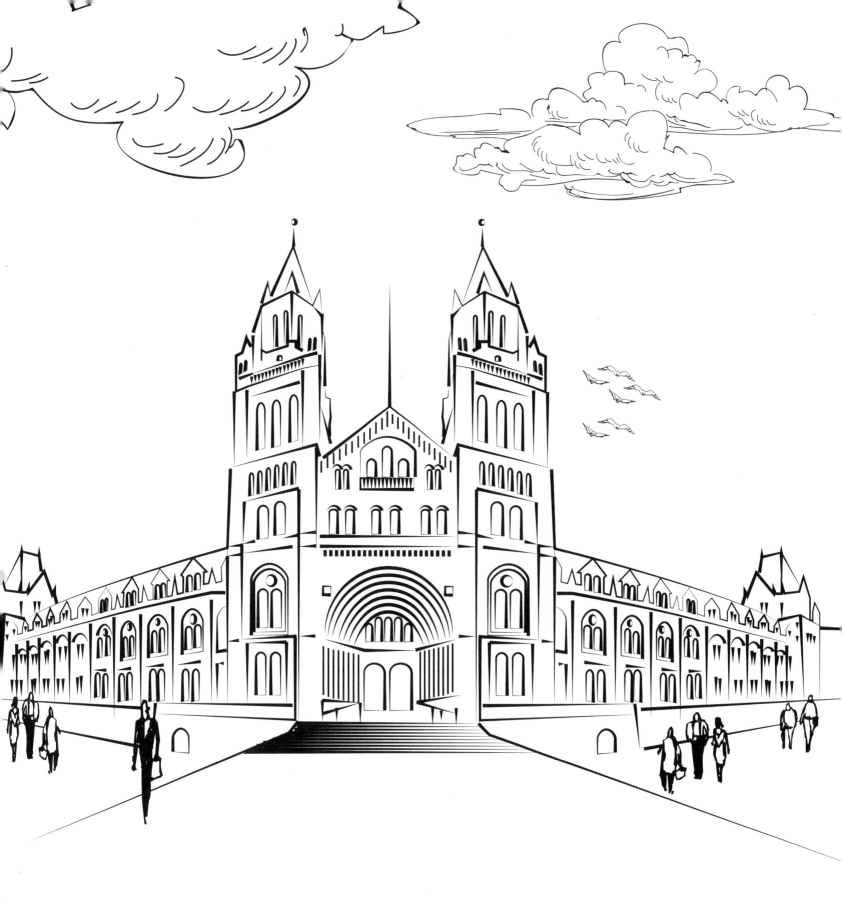

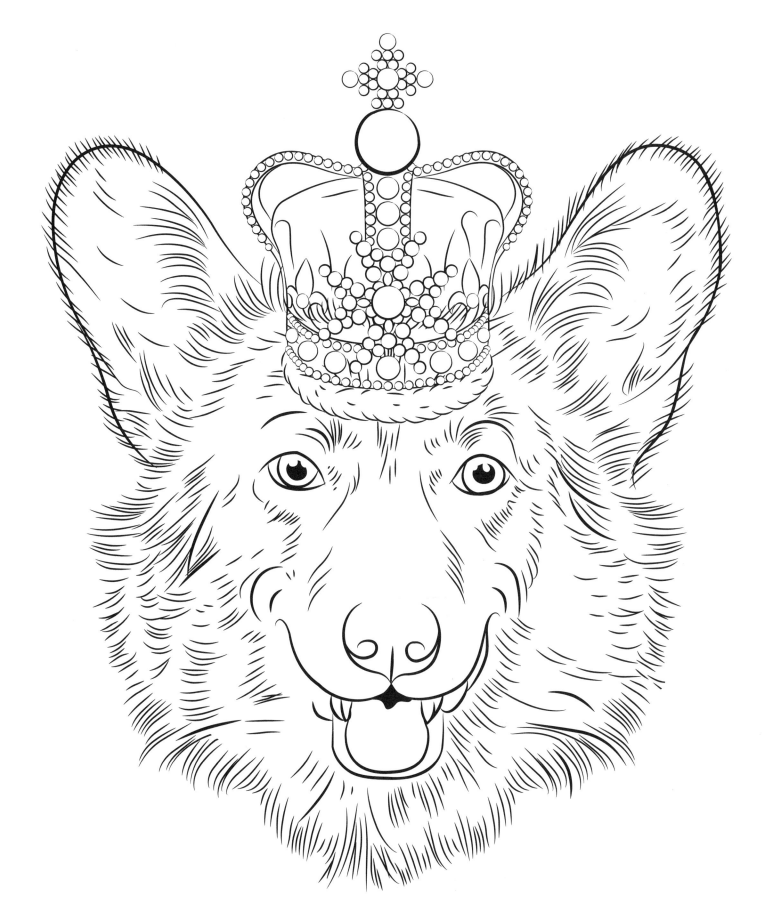

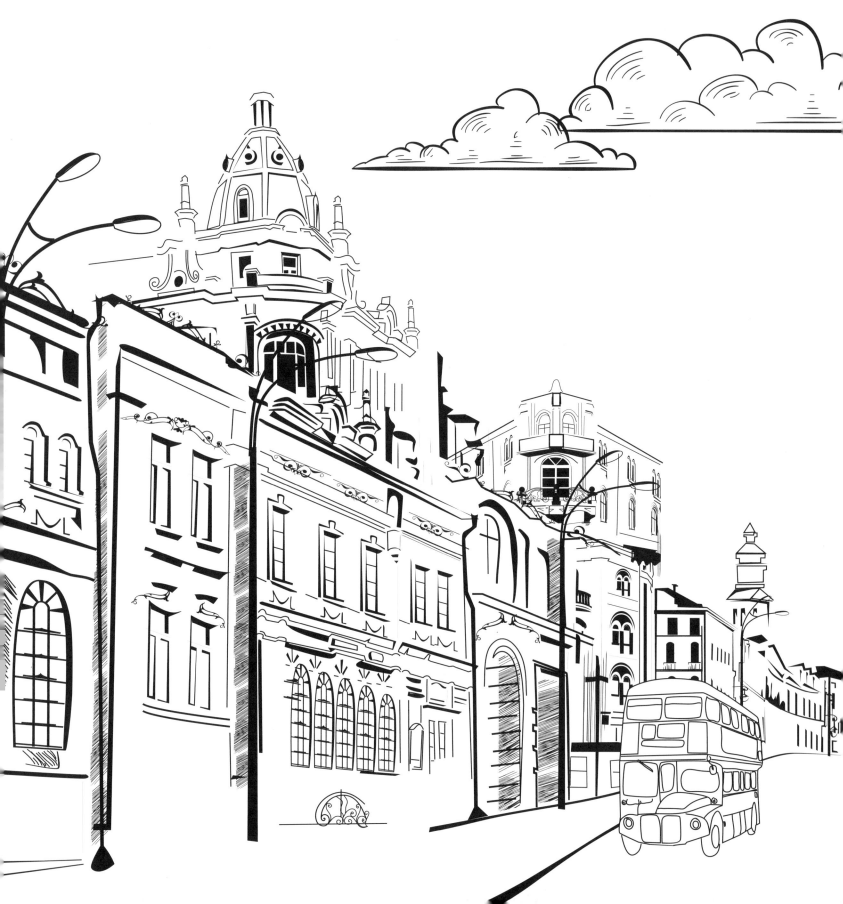

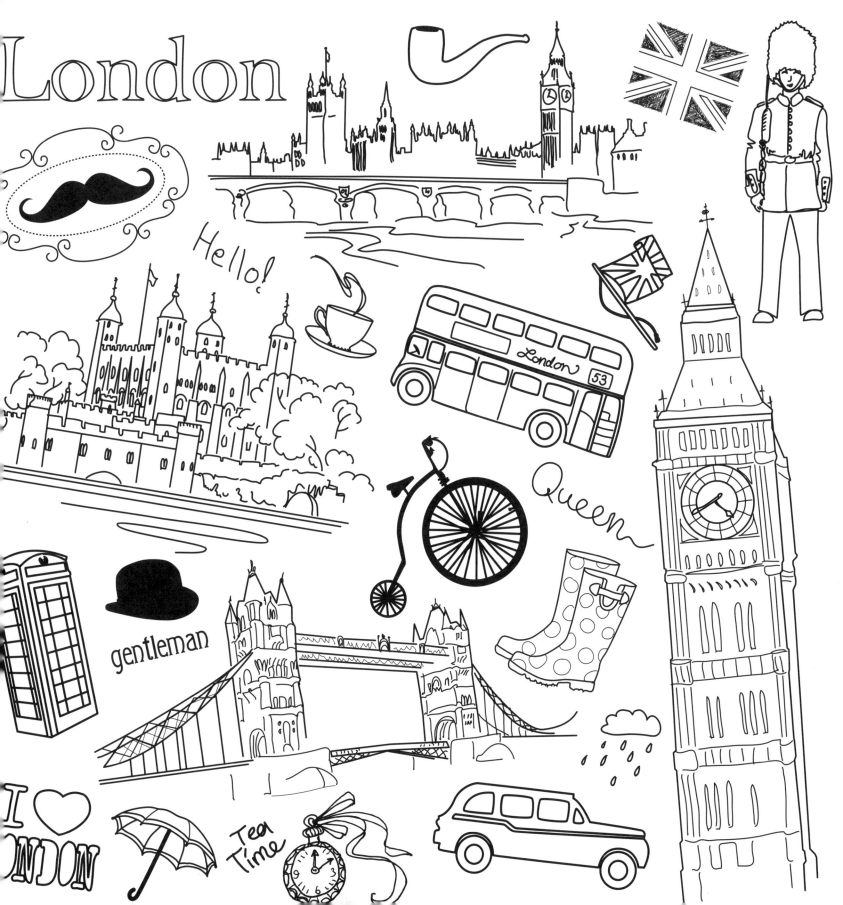

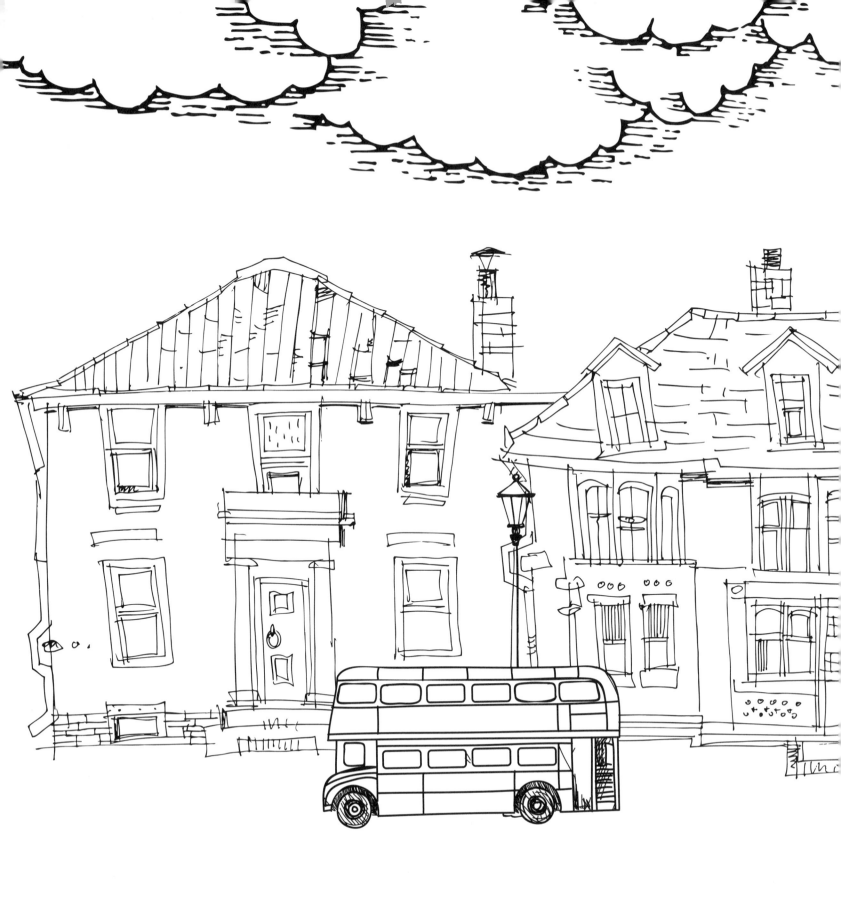

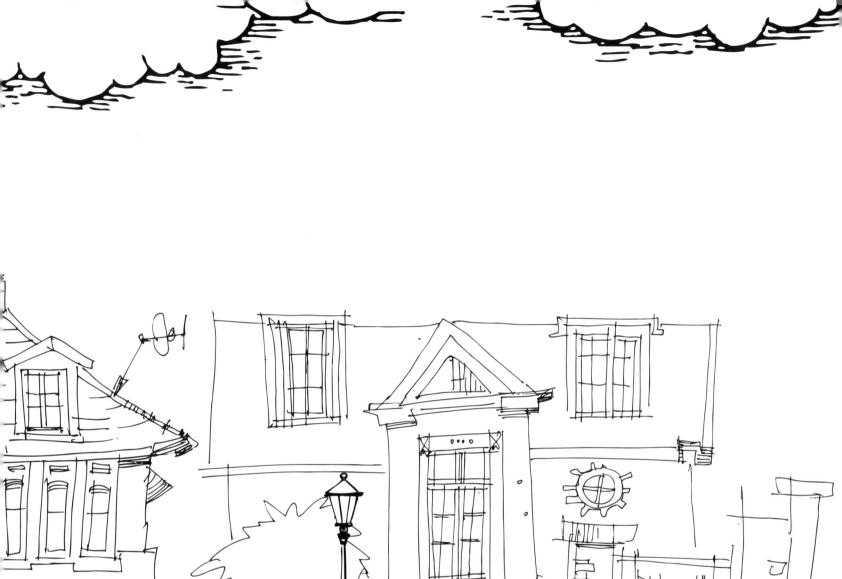

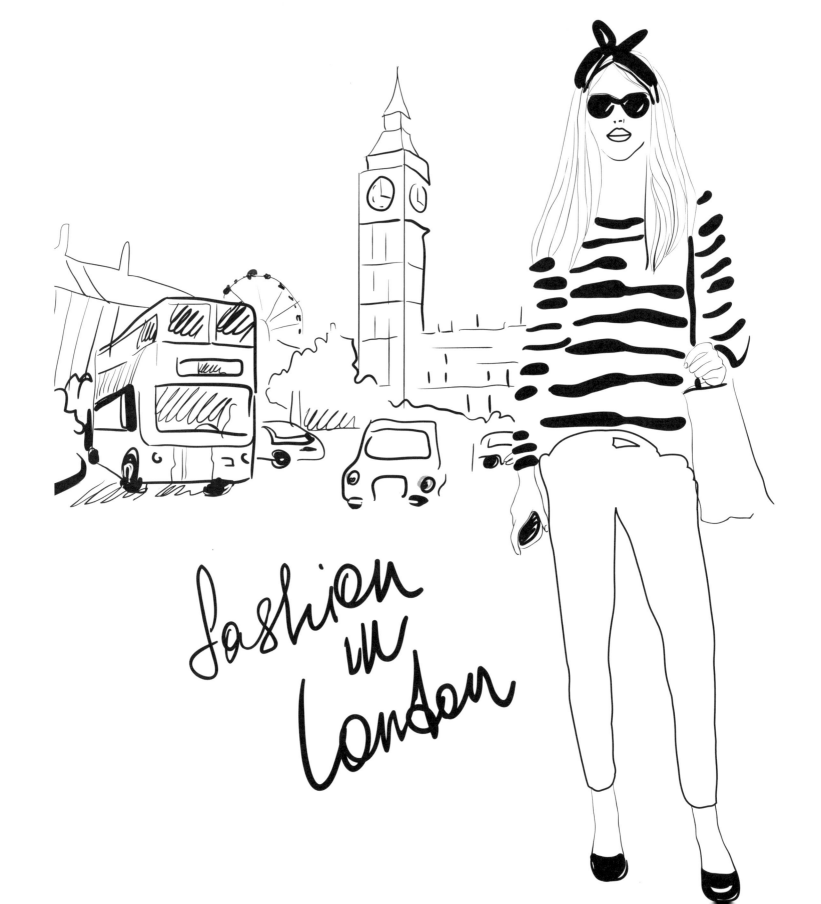

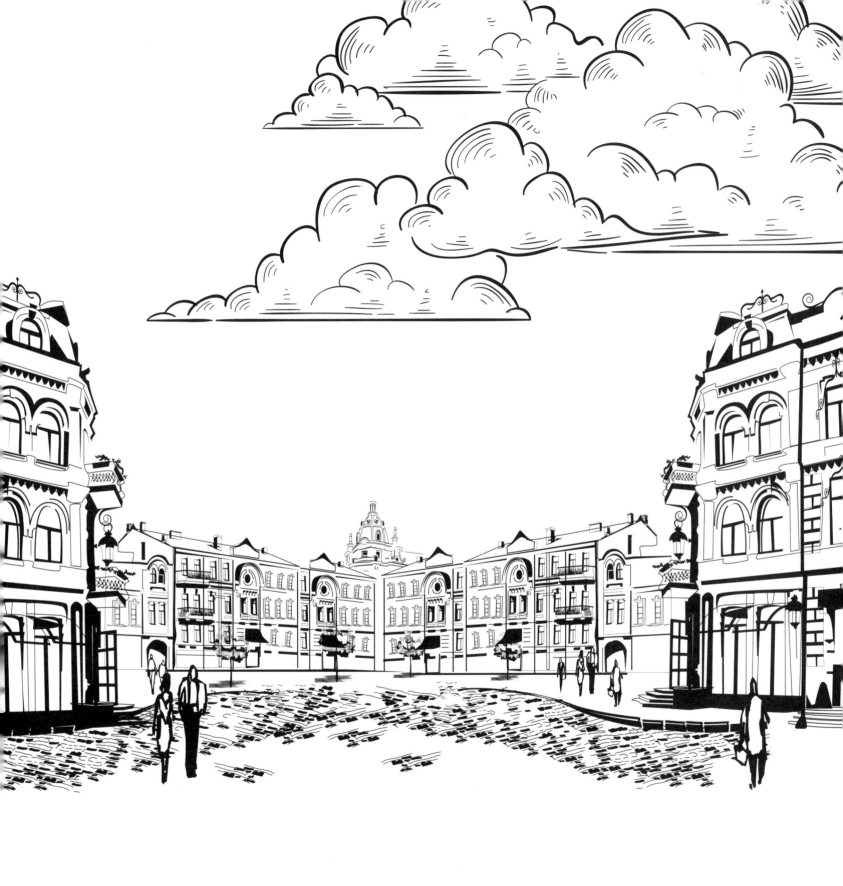

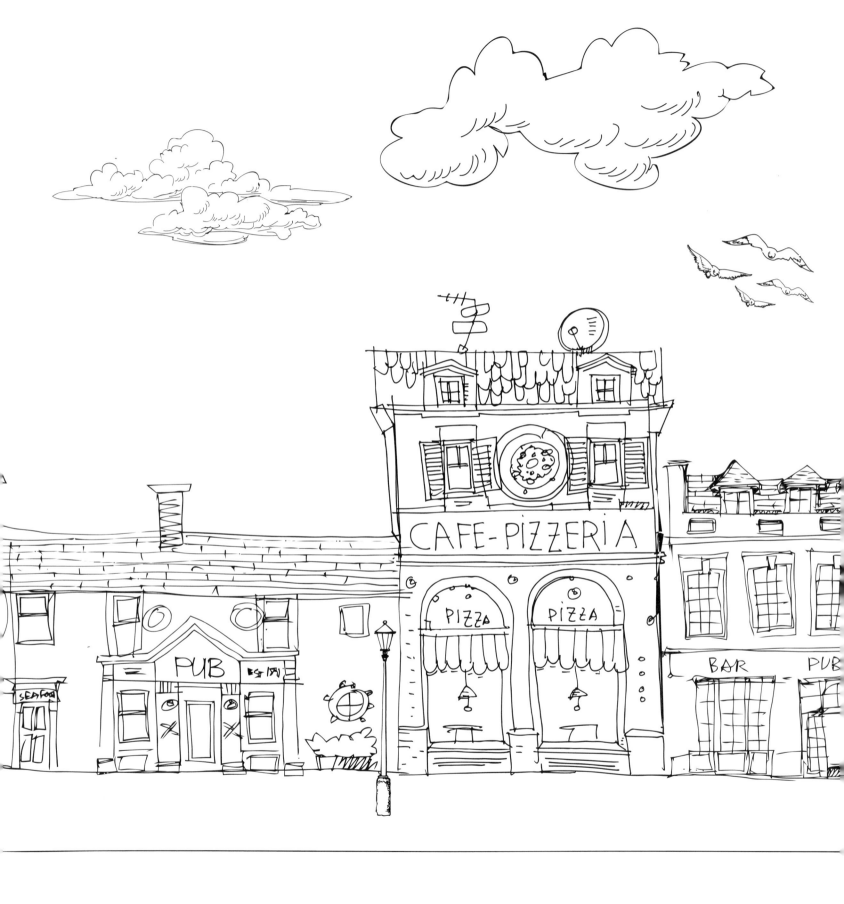

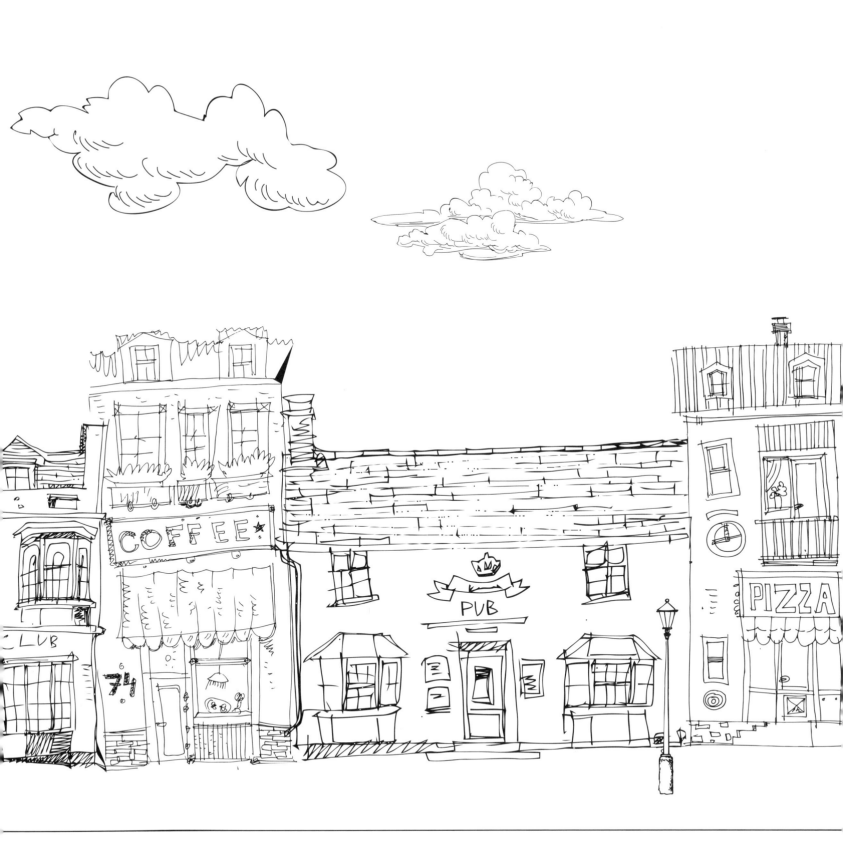

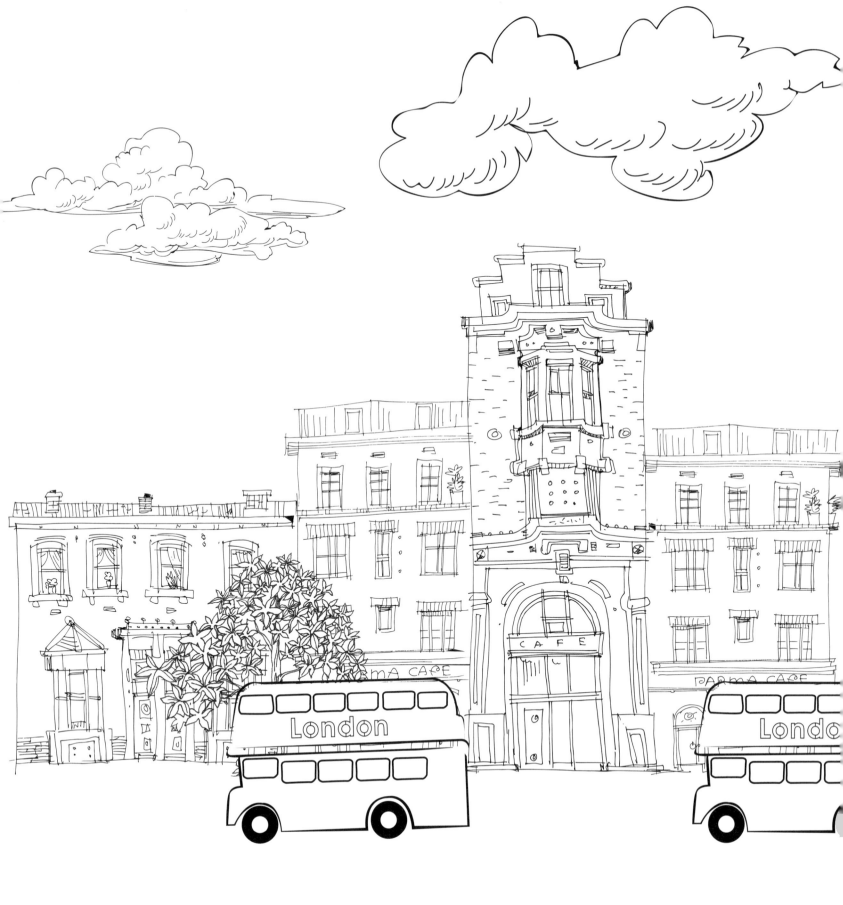

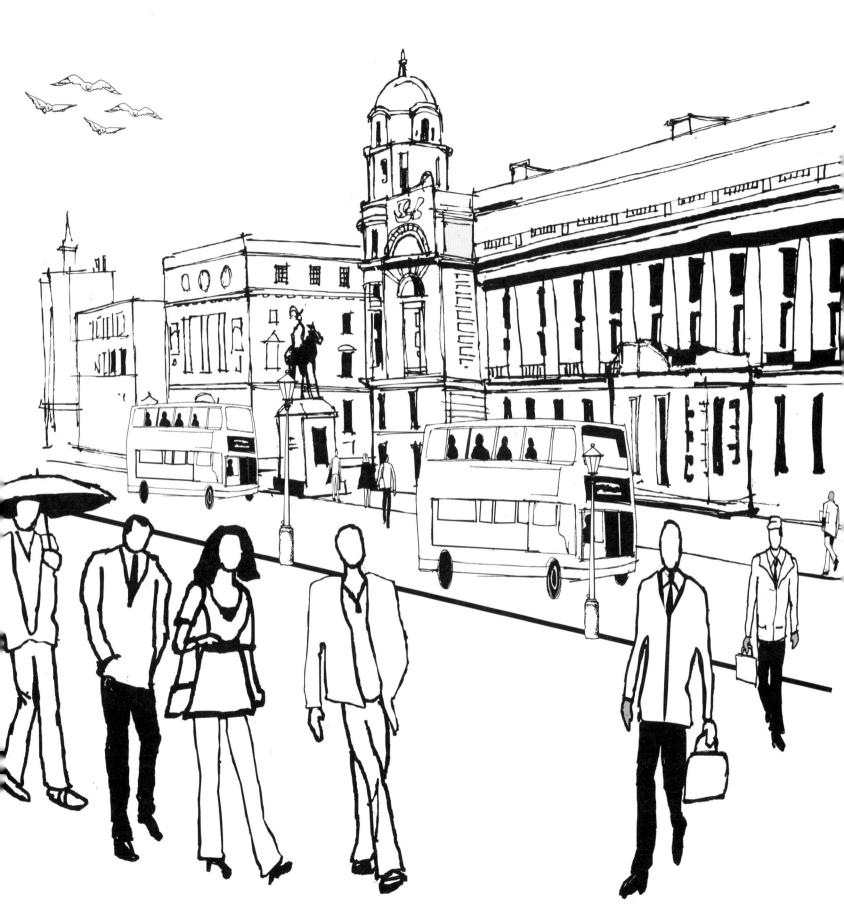

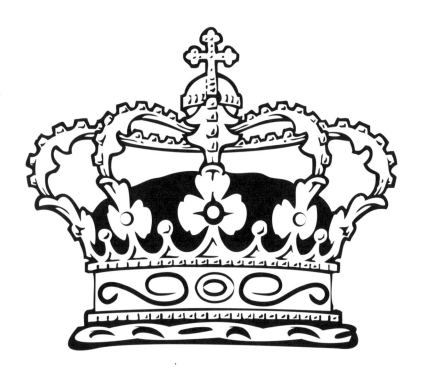
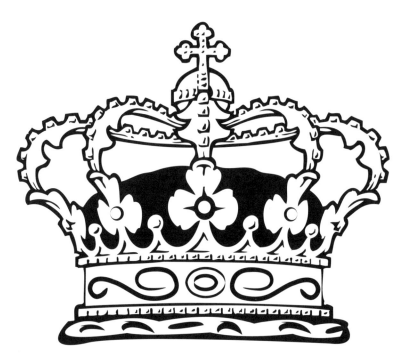
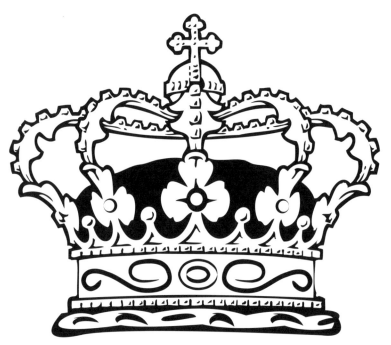
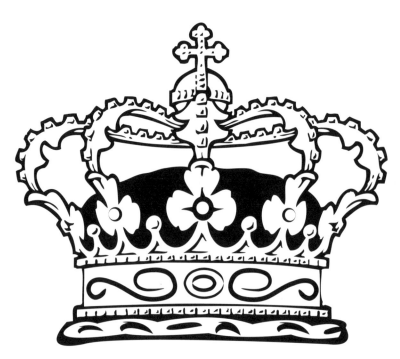

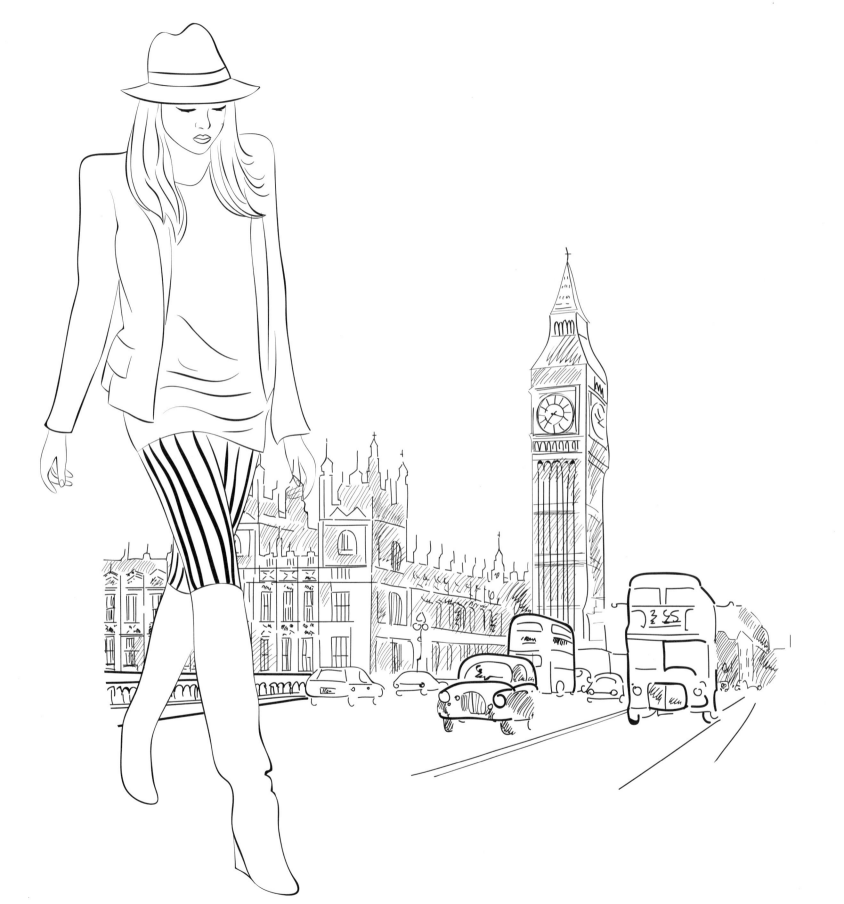

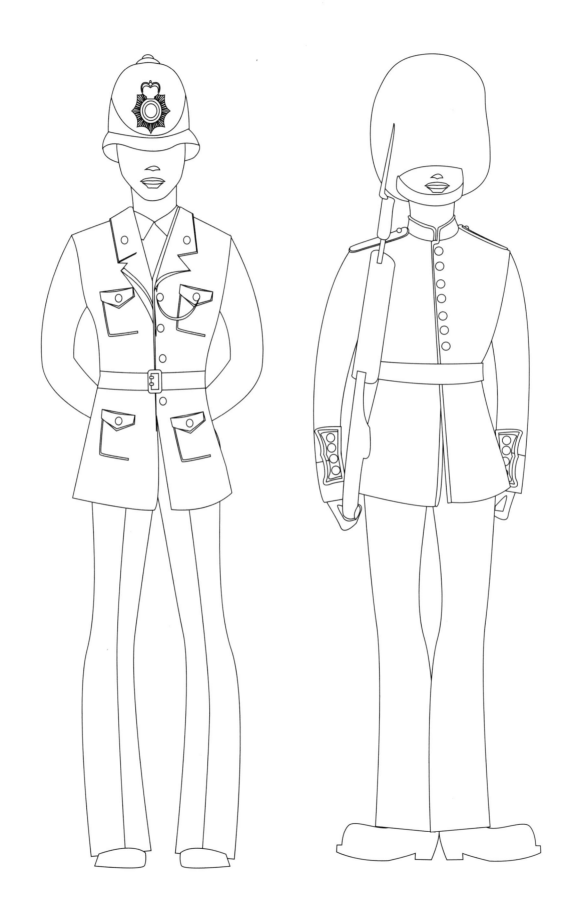

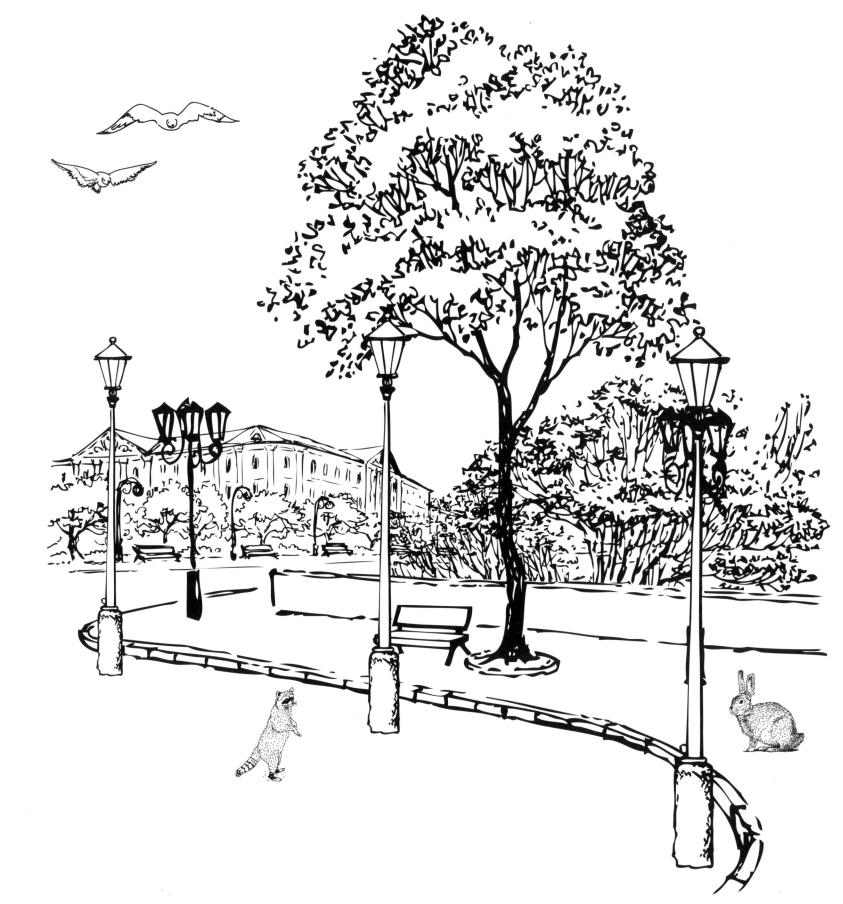

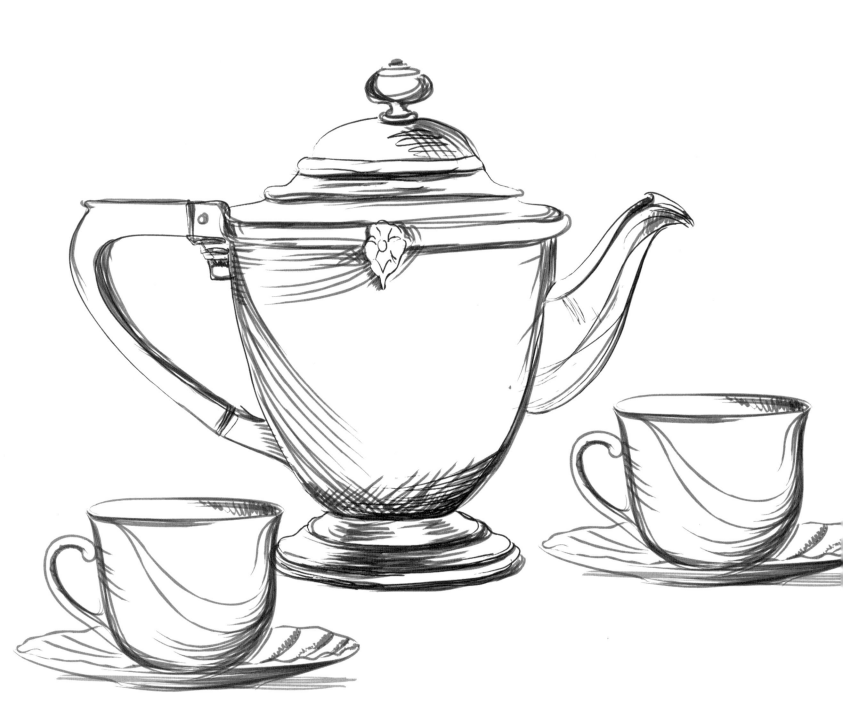

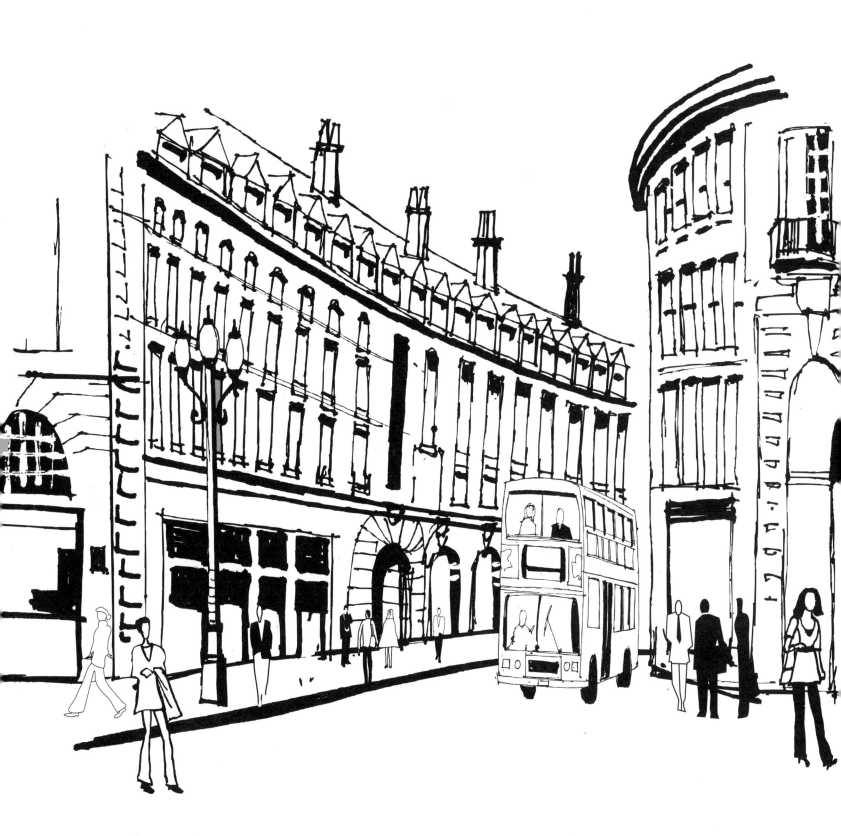

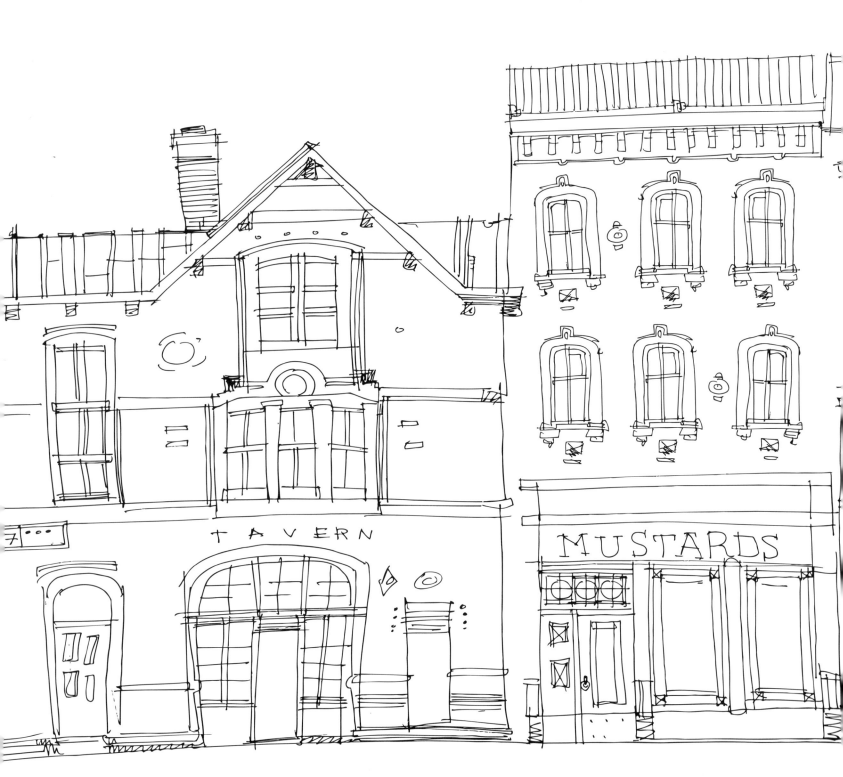

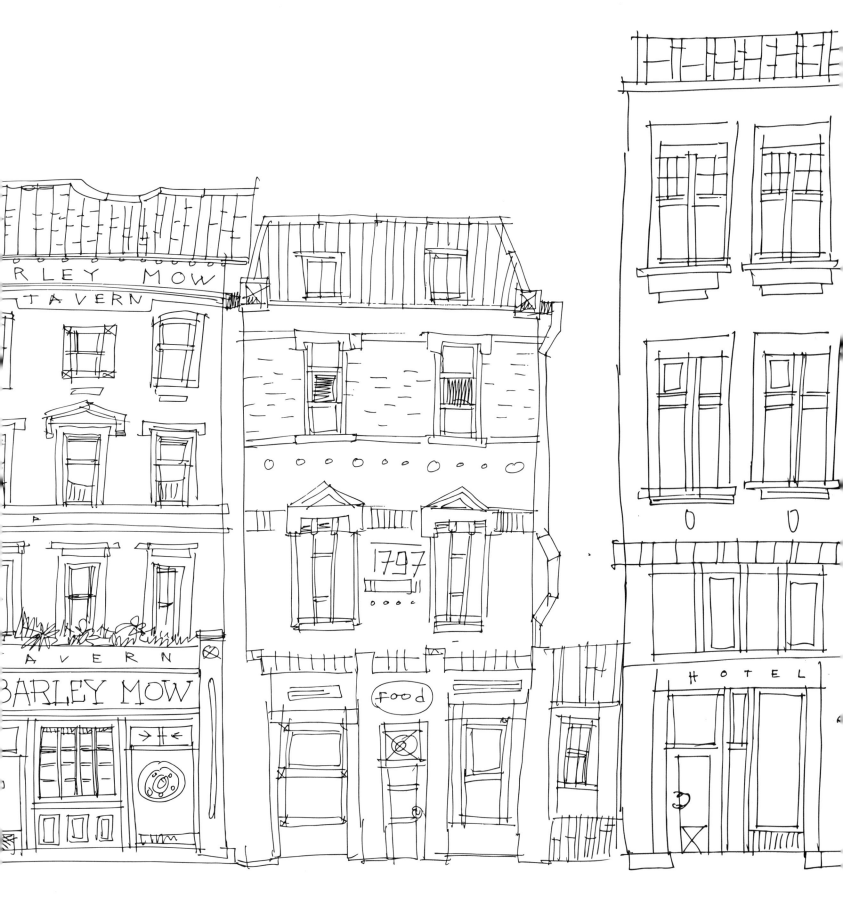

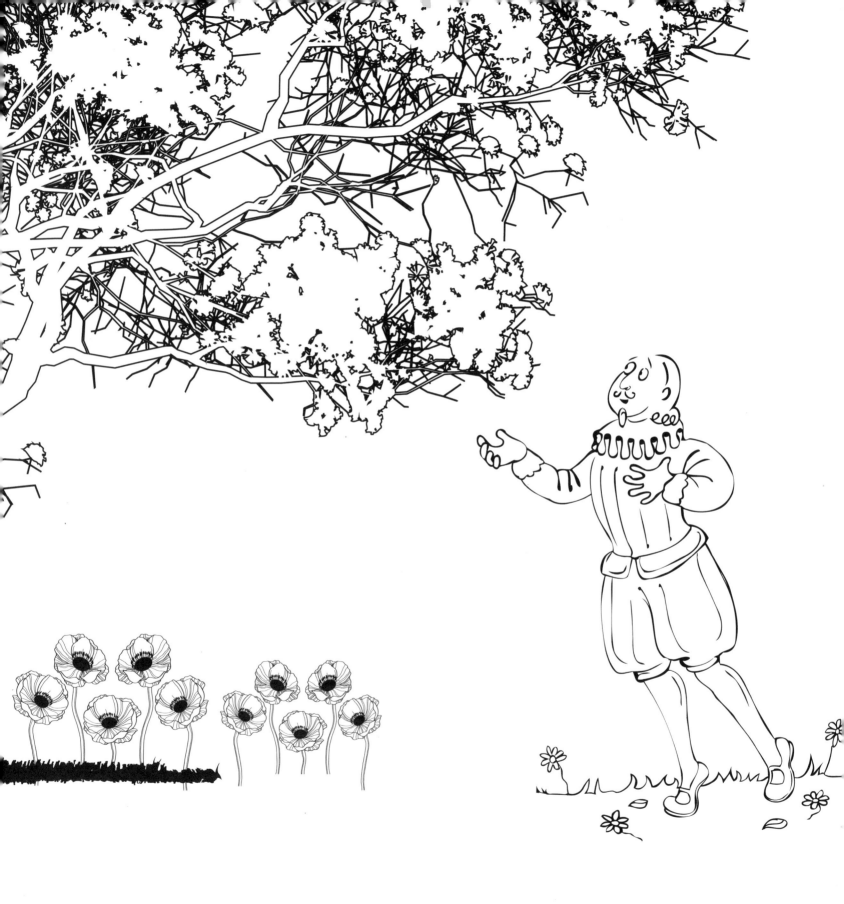

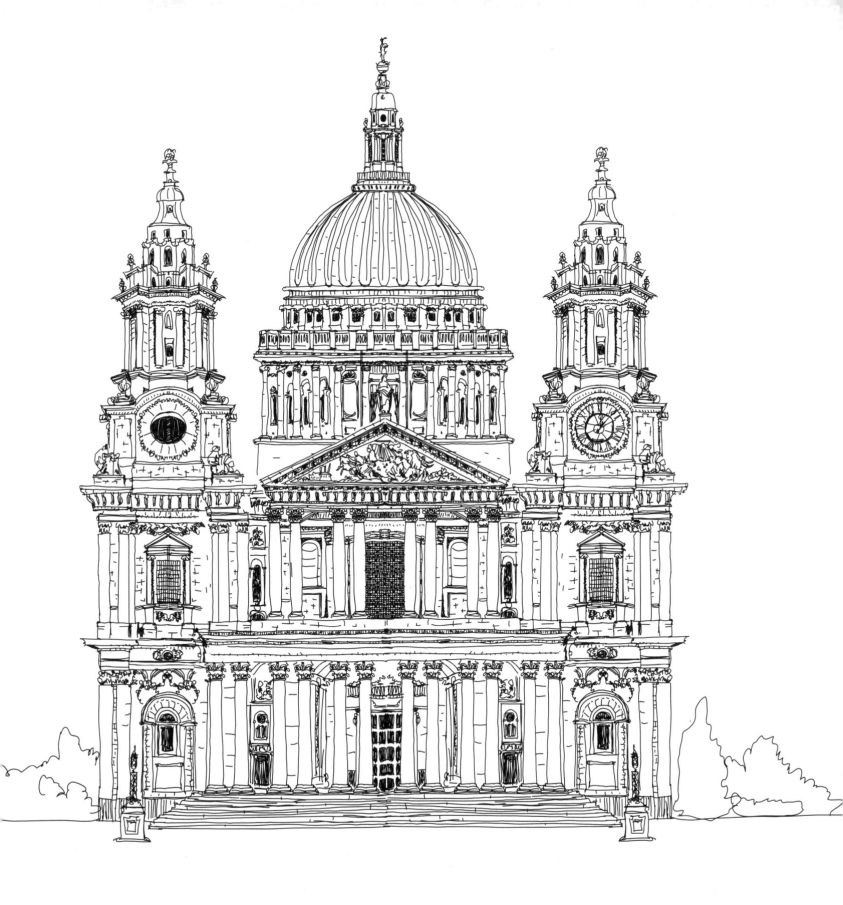

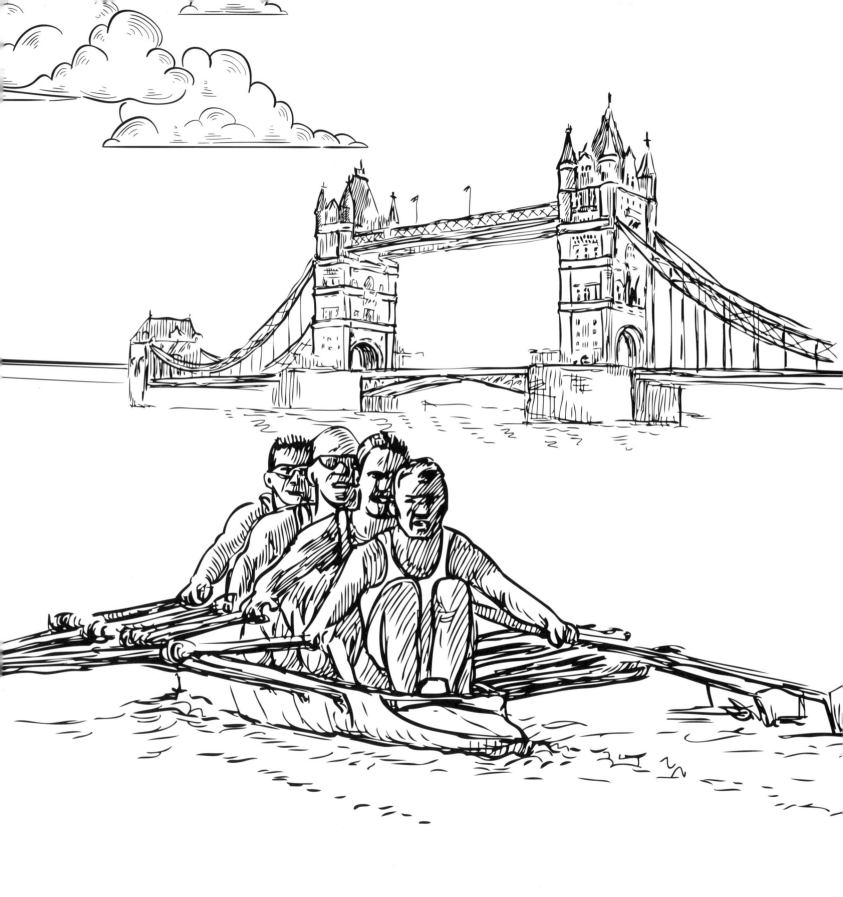

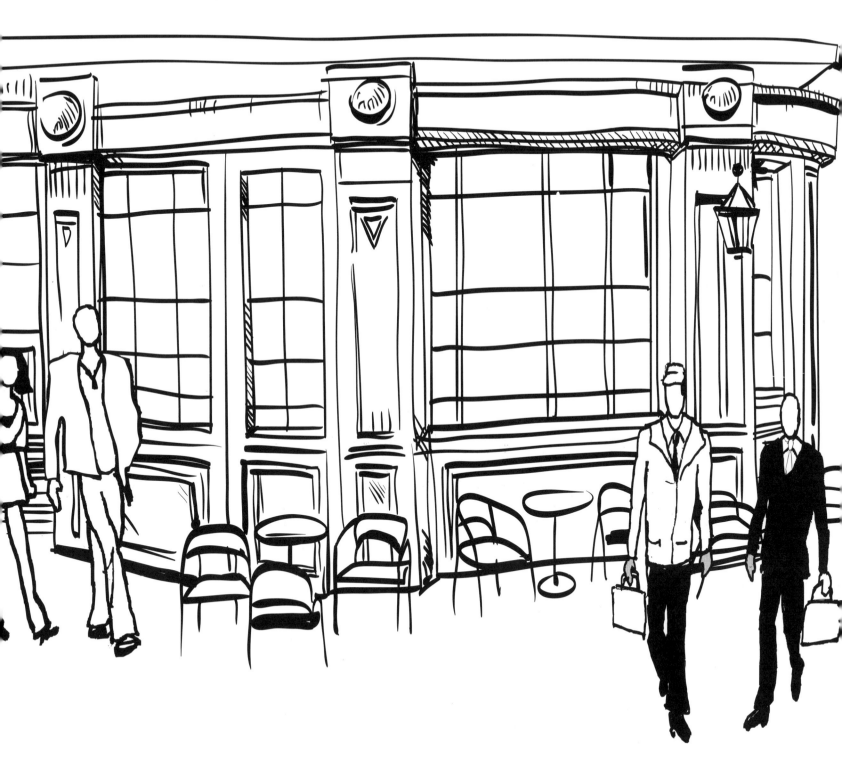

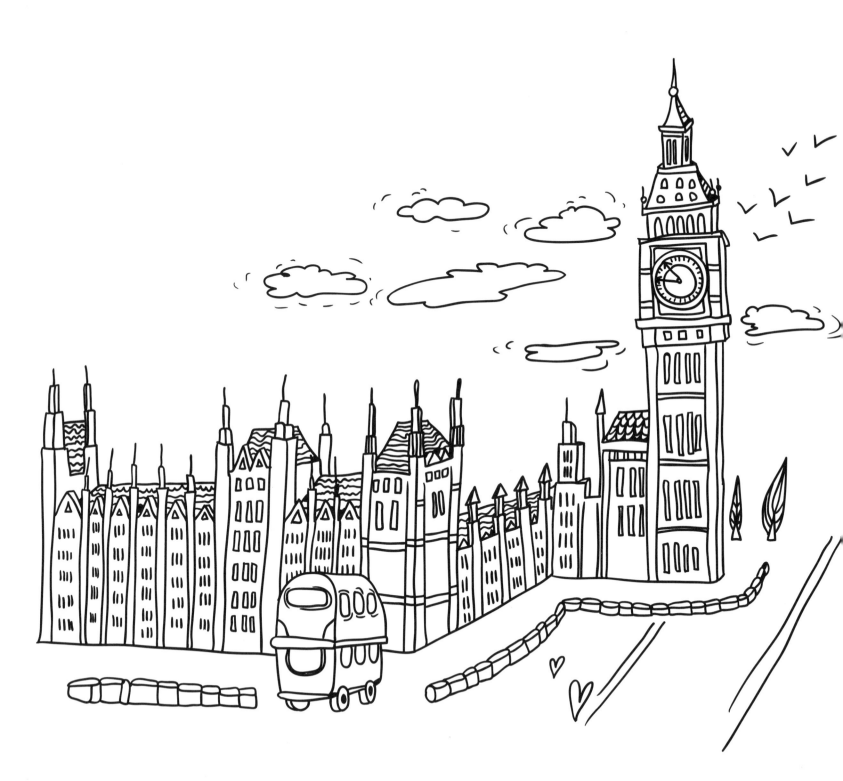

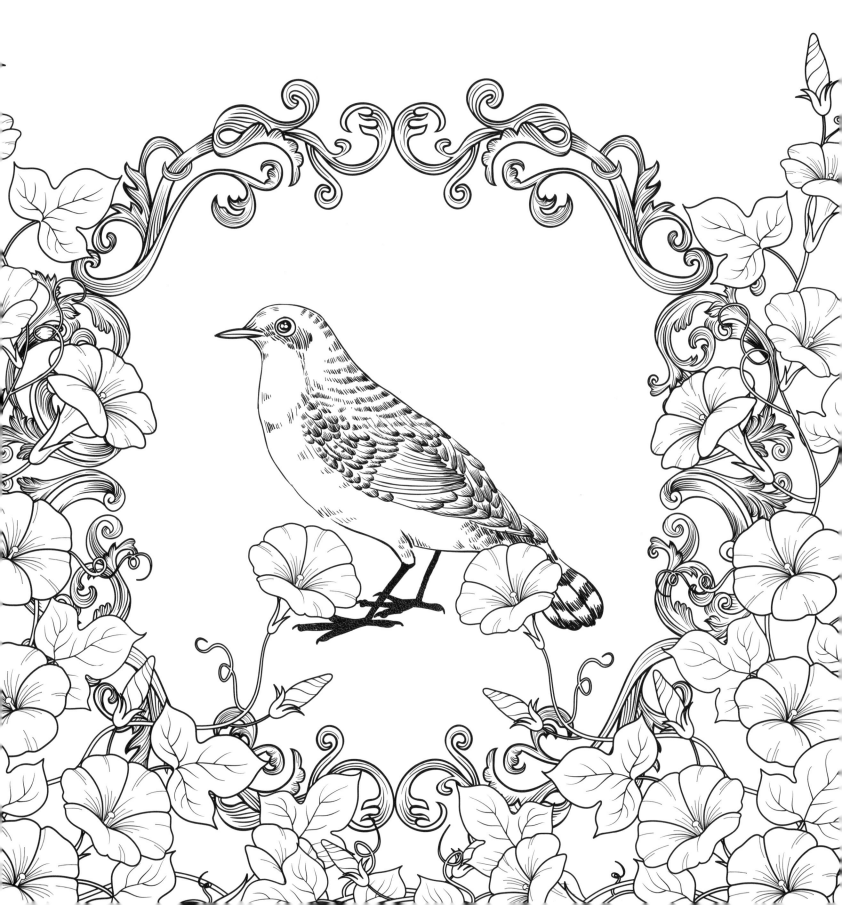

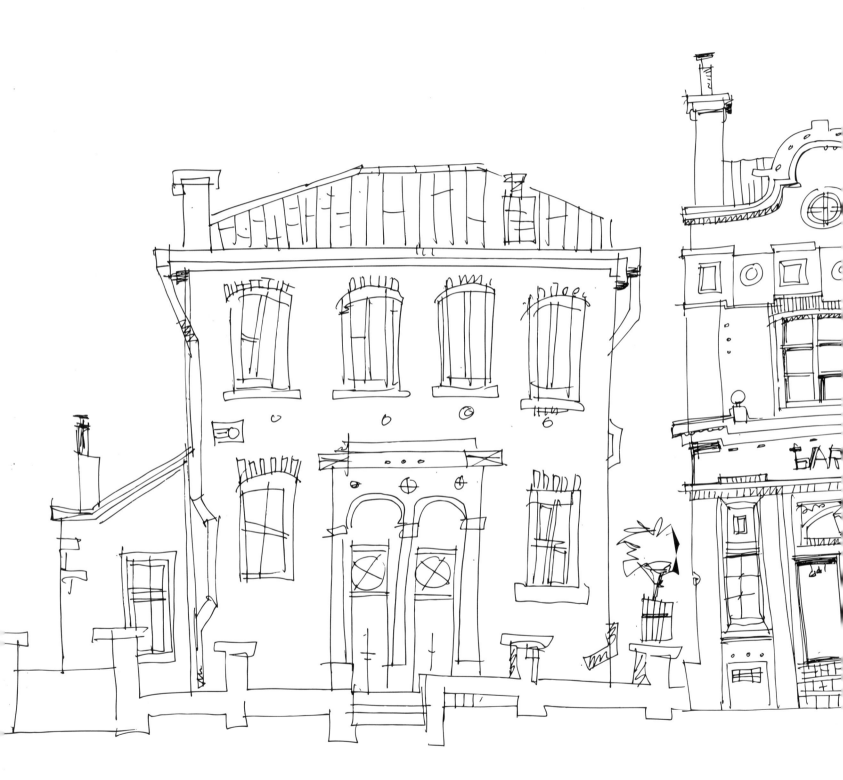

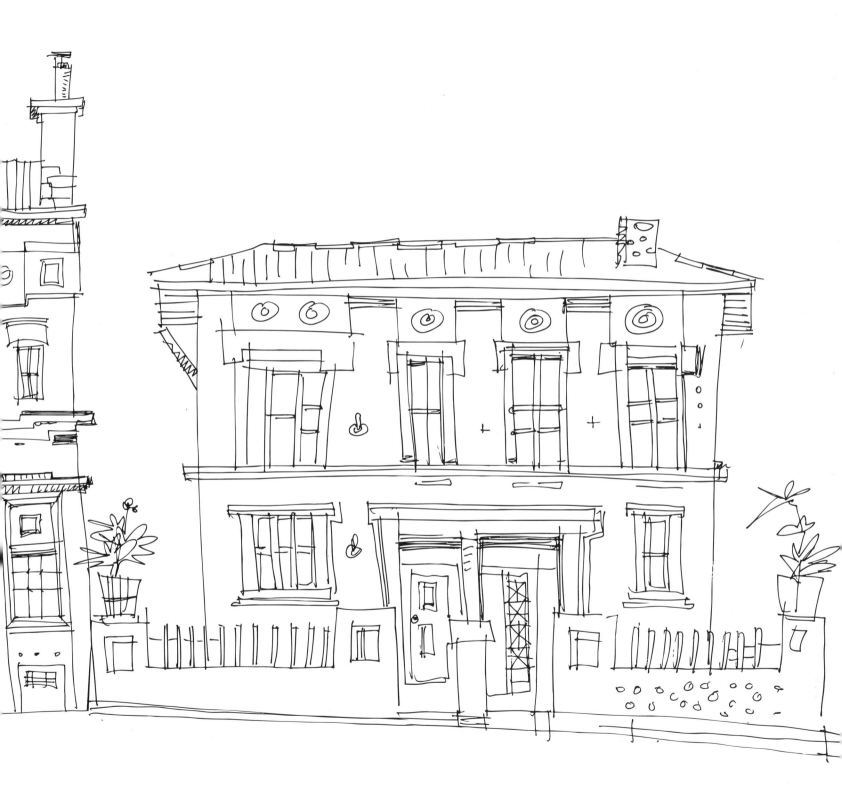

First published in 2015 by New Holland Publishers Pty Ltd
London • Sydney • Auckland

The Chandlery Unit 009 50 Westminster Bridge Road London SE1 7QY United Kingdom
1/66 Gibbes Street Chatswood NSW 2067 Australia
Office no 5 39 Woodside Ave Northcote, Auckland 0627, New Zealand

www.newhollandpublishers.com

Copyright © 2015 New Holland Publishers Pty Ltd
Copyright © 2015 in images: Shutterstock

All rights reserved. No part of this publication may be reproduced, stored in a retrieval system or
transmitted, in any form or by any means, electronic, mechanical, photocopying, recording or otherwise,
without the prior written permission of the publishers and copyright holders.

A record of this book is held at the British Library and the National Library of Australia.

ISBN 9781742577418

Managing Director: Fiona Schultz
Designer: Andrew Quinlan
Production Director: Olga Dementiev
Printer: Toppan Leefung Printing Ltd

10 9 8 7 6 5 4 3 2 1

Keep up with New Holland Publishers on Facebook
www.facebook.com/NewHollandPublishers